Dance For
Your Daddy

Dance For Your Daddy

KATHERINE SHELLDUCK

EBURY
PRESS

5 7 9 10 8 6 4

Published in 2007 by Ebury Press
an imprint of Ebury Publishing
A Random House Group Company

First published in Australia by Fremantle Arts Centre Press
in 2005 as *Desperate Hearts*

The Random House Group Limited Reg. No. 954009

Addresses for companies within the Random House Group can be
found at www.randomhouse.co.uk

A CIP catalogue record for this book
is available from the British Library

Printed in the UK by CPI Cox & Wyman, Reading, RG1 8EX

9780091921507

To Avalon and Orson
with love always

Contents

Winter 1968

Picture, if you will, a small child with greasy brown hair and a patch over one eye. The child is concentrating hard, the tip of her tongue compressed between her lips for added concentration. The child is bent on blasphemy because, in black letters, she has written on the wallpaper, 'I hate God.'

I wonder if the child's life would have been any different if she had written, 'I love God.'

I can wonder all I like for the child and I are one. And though we had only a vague notion of who 'God' might be, we knew that somehow He'd had a hand in things, and 'things' weren't exactly as they should be.

Emerging from my corner of spidery writings, I find a magnificent breakfast laid out and waiting for me. This is an exaggeration; there's a cereal packet in the cupboard. I am glad though, because it's Rice Krispies. (Snap, crackle and pop!) I pull up a seat at our wonky formica table.

I lay out a bowl, a spoon, milk and sugar. I pour the Rice Krispies into my bowl and carefully add the milk and sugar.

Then I lower my ear to listen. Sure enough, just like the ad on the telly. Snap! Crackle! Pop!

Smack!

My father has crept up on me. He knocks the spoon from my hand and sends it spinning across the table.

'What do I tell you fuckin' gurls? You don't look after nuffink.'

I blink in surprise. Well, my good eye blinks, the other one with the plaster over it may not have.

'You fuckin' bent the spoon!'

My father towers over me, his green eyes blazing. Oh he's angry. He picks up my bowl and chucks it over me. My breakfast splatters everywhere. Uh-oh, I think, there goes my bowl of Rice Krispies with the perfectly applied sugar-to-milk ratio.

I look up, which is a mistake really. Never make eye contact at times like this. Never speak. But I can't help myself.

'I didn't do it!'

Smack!

This time he knocks me off my chair. I feel a surge of righteous indignation because I am innocent. I haven't bent the spoon.

To be honest I haven't even noticed its crookedness. I had been looking forward to eating my Rice Krispies with it. I am in fact indifferent to its imperfect curvature. My father isn't.

I see his hand come up to hit me again and I try to dodge it, but it catches me. My indignation is replaced by fear.

My father forces my head down and rubs my face in the

mess. I breathe in milk, sugar, Rice Krispies. I open my mouth to scream, but no sound comes out.

'Fuckin' ugly little fuckin' cripple. You can forget about breakfast and you can fuckin' clear that up.'

(I should note here that my father can't stand physical imperfection of any kind. I am certainly not up to standard as, in addition to a partially blind eye, I have a condition called talipes, which causes me to walk on my toes.)

As suddenly as my father appeared, he's gone.

I sit up and review the damage. 1) I am alive, that's good. 2) I might be able to salvage my breakfast.

Number two doesn't eventuate, because my father comes back in and orders me to stand in the corner with a book on my head. This is one of his favourite punishments, which he says will fix my feet and improve my posture.

'Fuckin' keep it on your fick 'ead until I tell you.'

The book is red, large like an encyclopaedia, and weighs a ton. I hold it balanced on my bonce until my arms ache and I feel my neck bending under the weight like a flower stem. I know from experience that I will have to wait until he either loses interest or goes out before I am reprieved.

Please understand, I've got nothing against books, on the contrary, I love them. But as a rule I prefer reading them to weighing them on my head.

Apart from my parents I have a wonderful family. I'd like you to meet my sisters: they have nicknames. My father started it with 'Bud', short for Rosebud. Bud is older than me by two years and the bossiest girl in the whole of

Christendom. Between ourselves we call her Mrs Grimnasty. Bud is short, with curly brown hair and green eyes, which are fairly mesmerising. They're carbon copies of my father's, that's why. She'll look after you if you are sick and box your ears if you are not.

My twin sister Tigs is partly bald and hardly talks at all. She likes peppermints, not chocolate, and generally likes her food to crunch. Tigs is about as shy a girl as you would want to meet. Though you wouldn't meet her because she'd be hiding behind the fence, she doesn't like strangers. This might imply that she isn't smart. She is but she is also very cautious. Tigs goes to bed every night with her football. She's been called Tigs ever since I can remember and nobody can say why.

My youngest sister Lu (short for Lucille) is the one you'd really fall in love with. She's a spectacular beauty, with olive skin and hazel eyes and thick lustrous hair. A tropical flower of extraordinary beauty. If you're out with Lu, people stop you in the street and give you sweets. Don't let her good looks fool you though; Lu is the cleverest of us by far. I don't think it does her any good, because behind those hazel eyes, I can see her thinking and if you think too much you start to worry and where's that going to lead? To the loony bin, and we've got enough loonies in the family.

My mother you'd like to see. She looks like Snow White. She's the most beautiful mother around. I've seen other fathers looking at her, only they'd never dare come near because my father would kill them. 'I'll fuckin' kill 'em and then I'll fuckin' kill you.' He threatens this frequently, which is how I know.

My mother never eats, she drinks cups of tea. She winds her slim fingers round the stem of her cup and sips. When we're out, waiting for a bus or something, sometimes she'll sigh, 'I'd love a cup of tea.' I don't understand this tea business, I've tried it and it's not up to much. Tizer is a superior drink, in my opinion.

When I ask my mother where we all came from, she smiles. She says one day she was taking the rubbish out and came upon us all by accident, under the potato peelings and tea-leaves.

Lu gets upset over this as she is sure she could not possibly come from such lowly origins. Lu believes she doesn't really come from our family at all and has been placed here by mistake. She expects her real family to roll up in a carriage and pick her up any day.

My nanny is my mother's mother. She does her best to weather the storms. But too much bad weather has taken its toll. If you ask her if she's not well, she'll deny it, but sometimes I catch her leaning on a chair.

You can talk to my nanny about anything. She's got an open mind and she's a very good mimic. Lurking in the family we have some deaf and dumb relatives, and she can imitate them trying to answer the telephone. I think you'd have to see this performance yourself to see the funny side; even the deaf and dumb relatives laugh like hell.

When I think about my nanny I get an ache in my heart. I always say to her, 'Nanny, when I'm big I'll do this for you

… buy that for you, go there with you …' But she looks at me with her sad eyes, as if she knows the future and that my dreams may never come true.

There you have us, the main characters in my little drama. One father, one mother, a nanny, three sisters and me. Cobblestones of memory, seen through my one good eye. Now I am an adult, then I was a child. The two voices that are me.

It is winter. Tigs and I are eight years old and I am by the stair in the hall watching my father coming through the door. He has dark, slicked-back hair; he's wearing a suit, with a vest underneath like a shirt. He looks as handsome as can be. You can smell my dad even before you see him, he smells clean, like shaving soap. Tigs, always quick with the reflexes, makes herself scarce in the bedroom cupboard. I'm too slow, I've been spotted – but it's okay, Daddy seems to be in a positive mood.

'Point yer ears towards me and shut your cakehole.'

He's carrying cardboard boxes inside and stacking them in the lounge. He lines the family up to announce his new project. We stand side by side like the girls in *The Sound of Music*, only without the sailor dresses and the big house. Bud stands to attention, clear eyes analysing the situation. Tigs bites her lips, Lu glances at me and I look at the carpet. My mother flicks back her long hair.

He opens the first box: dozens of miniature perfume bottles about an inch high.

'You get the bottles, then you fill 'em up with the perfume from 'ere.'

Father bangs a drum of liquid.

'Then you screw up the lids an' stick on the labels. Don't spill any. Got it?'

We nod, because even if we haven't we know that asking questions means asking for trouble.

'They better be done by the time I get back.'

My father exits, leaving Mummy and us and a million tiny bottles.

At first we think it's fun because the little bottles are cute, but they don't fill quickly due to the stoppers, then the sickly smell starts to make us feel ill and the taste of the glue from the labels shrivels our tongues.

Our mother tries to make it seem like a game, but underneath we know that it's more than our lives are worth not to finish the job.

Bedtime comes and goes. The clock ticks on and on. The bottles seem like they'll never be filled. I rub my eyes, weary of the stink and the sight of them. The perfume stings my eyes and I start to cry. I want to go to sleep.

My mother looks at us. Lu is already asleep, curled up like a hamster. Her eyes closed, her lashes make perfect semi-circles on her flushed cheeks.

'Go to bed,' she says. 'You've done enough. I'll finish them off, it won't take me long.'

We know it will, because there are still boxes and boxes left.

Tigs and I look at each other in relief. Tigs looks even paler than usual, she has dark rings under her eyes but you

would never hear her complain. Bud looks from us to
our mother.

'You go. I'll stay and help Mummy,' Bud nods her curly
head at us. We creep off to bed, feeling guilty.

In the morning the bottles are filled and stacked neatly
with their black and gold labels winking, 'Chanel No. 5'.
My father is pleased, though he doesn't actually say so. He
grunts. (That's a good sign.) Mummy and Bud look grey
with tiredness.

We all reek of perfume for days. I call the stuff Chanel
Stink-O.

I give a bottle of it to the lady from the mobile library
and she looks at me suspiciously and asks where I got it
from. 'Miss,' I say, 'I got it from my father. He makes it.' At
that, she looks very closely at the label and then back at me.
'Does he indeed?'

Ah yes. That's not all, I want to say. This morning I found
this bag. I had been looking for sweets. I am an expert at
sneaking them from under people's noses. I put my hand in
the bag and felt a sticky liquid on my fingers, then I looked
at it. A red smear. Then I looked in the bag: bloody knives
and clothes. It didn't feel good. What did it mean? I don't
know. There are no answers; I daren't ask the questions.

Bad bag. Bad blood. Bad men? Maybe it's linked to the
bad men who visit.

They came before, when we were still living in the caravan park. It was a fine day and Nanny had come over to
help my mother do the washing. You had to queue to take
your turn at the taps.

There were signs up about the laundry and every other human activity. Things like:

STRICTLY NO POTATO PEELINGS
OR PEA PODS IN THE DRAINS
DO NOT WASTE WATER
NO RADIOS AFTER 10 PM
CLEANLINESS is next to GODLINESS.

We were outside hanging out the washing with Nanny when two men arrived looking for my father. They were ever so polite, standing there in their camel overcoats and black leather gloves. One of them had a red stain on his cuff, just half an inch around the top. Maybe he'd had a nosebleed?

They wished us good morning, and asked if we'd seen Ted.

Through their legs I saw my father returning from the shower block. (I'll say this for my father, you'd never find him unwashed even on his worst day.) Father took one look at the men and went pale as a Nestle's Milky Bar. I'd never seen him run so fast.

Nanny saw him run too, but she didn't miss a beat. She made out she wouldn't mind seeing my father herself, 'seeing as he's run off and left my daughter with four hungry mouths to feed. If you find him,' she said, 'give him one for me.' The way she said it you'd think she really meant it.

The two men thought it was funny. They slapped their leather gloves on their thighs and laughed. 'Not to worry,' they said. 'Tell him it's business.' They turned and left, driving off in their shiny car.

As soon they had disappeared people poured from their caravans and started carrying on. Curious, I asked Nanny if the men were famous or something, and Nanny said that in a way they were. They were famous for being very bad. The Kray Twins.

It meant nothing to me, but the distraction was a chance to get out of helping with the wash and sneak off to see Mavis and Bert.

Mavis gives me big slabs of her homemade cake. They have a vegetable garden and roses around their caravan. Bert shows me his stump, which he got from the war. His foot got blown off by a mine. If you ask him he'll tell you all about it. How in the mornings he can still feel his foot like a ghost. His Ghost Foot. I tell him, 'I've seen it.' Skipping along the path in a red sock with the big toe peeping through.

We left the caravan park soon after the Kray visit – somehow my father persuaded someone at the council that it was in everyone's best interests to let us jump the queue for a council house.

We packed up our belongings very hastily while my father went to 'sort out' the caravan park caretaker who was bothering him over the small matter of rent owing.

Our house is identical to all the other council houses on the estate, except that it has a different-coloured door. Ours is blue, next door's is red. Father says, 'I don't like the look of 'em, they're probably fuckin' commies.' Mind you, it has to be said, our father's never liked the look of any neighbours.

Nevertheless, I make friends with the reds' daughter, Cheryl. Lu and I play with Cheryl every day.

At mealtimes, Cheryl's mum comes to the door in her curlers and yells, 'Cheryl! Cheryl!' You can hear it for miles.

Cheryl is shy, she goes red at the drop of a hat. The boys on the estate make fun of her. Lu and I never make fun of Cheryl because she is dying. Cheryl has heart disease. It runs in her family.

Now and again, to help Cheryl practise dying, we play funerals. Our plastic laundry basket is the coffin, which is unsatisfactory because whoever's playing dead has to dangle their legs over the side.

'Do you think dying is going to hurt?' Cheryl asks.

I think to myself that it will probably hurt like hell, but I can't bring myself to say that to Cheryl's face.

'I believe,' I say knowingly, 'it's more like getting tired and going to sleep.'

'Seeing as you're dying, can we have your *Girls' Own Annual*?'

Cheryl says, 'Okay.'

I like annuals. I like the story called 'No Tears for Molly', about a poor servant girl who's always being picked on by Pickering, the cruel butler. Molly is always pictured on her hands and knees in her maid's uniform, sobbing into a grate or some such. It's a surprise when you turn the page and see her standing up. She wears black stockings.

All the adults wore black when Cheryl died. They came for her body in a black car and took her off in a little white coffin. I didn't say goodbye. But I wanted to know why they put her in such a little box, because there wasn't enough room in it for her to grow.

One day my father pulls up in his van and says he's 'picked up a piana'. My father often 'picked' things up, but a piano? This was something different.

Bud, Tigs, Lu and I gather round to admire the 'piana'. It's glossy and chestnut-brown, like a conker, with pearly keys.

Out in the street where it stands, Father sits down with the air of a real pianist and knocks off a couple of tunes. My mother comes out, he looks at her and starts to sing one of her favourite songs. My mother smiles; it's a rare sight.

Soon all the neighbours have gathered around, and before we know it, they're having a right old knees-up. The men have brought beer and the women are dancing. Cheryl's mum, still in black, weeps when my father plays 'You'll never walk alone' for her little girl.

We children dance round and round until we're sick and giddy from spinning. But still my father's fingers run up and down the keys, playing requests. I'm flabbergasted, I didn't know he was musical.

As it gets late, the men get drunker. When it's time to shift the piano, there's no one sober standing. The drunken men try to take the piano through the front door. I catch snippets of alcoholic reasoning.

'Shift the rear end, Ted.'

'To the left. No. No. To the right.'

'Up … a bit. No, down.'

''Ang on, 'ang on.'

Eventually, "'S no way. Not unless we knock the door-frame in.'

'Let's knock the front door in.'

My mother and the other women, in an uproar, intervene just as the men attempt a drunken charge at the door with the piano.

Finally it is agreed to leave the piano where it is and to shift it in the morning.

I fall asleep listening to the commotion and the magical music still ringing in my ears.

The next day I get up early thinking of the miraculous piana. The sun is still coming up over the roofs, but I can hear voices and cracking sounds from outside. I open the door to find some estate boys are bashing up the piano. They pull out its wooden innards and smash them against the wall.

My father, hearing the noise, runs out in his vest and drawers. But it's too late. The piano lies like a dead thing, its keys scattered all over the concrete like broken teeth. The estate boys run off; even they are too scared to face my father.

My father bends down to pick up a broken key. I expect him to swear and start making threats, but I'm astonished to see tears in his eyes. I scurry off before he can catch me looking.

Looking I am. Looking for my father. There he is in his white vest, pale and slim and handsome, bending over in the chilly morning air, crying over a broken piano. I understand now. Senseless and stupid. A beautiful thing destroyed.

There he is also, sitting in front of the telly, watching *Coronation Street* and scoffing Jacob's Cream Crackers, cheese and pickled onions. He is oblivious to the fact that upstairs we are planning a great escape. 'Mummy is leaving Daddy.' And not for the first time.

We stuff our dearest possessions into plastic carrier bags. It takes some doing persuading the cat to get into a carrier bag, I can tell you! We tiptoe down the stairs, listening to every guffaw coming from the lounge. As silent as snails (scared snails), we straggle out of the back door and into the night. My mother is at the helm, looking white and panicky.

It's cold and drizzling snow. Luckily we have our fake leopard-skin coats to wear against the weather. Our coats came from the 'back-of-a-lorry' shop, which is, my father says, 'where yer get yer discounts'.

Unfortunately, we have to wait an hour at the bus stop for the next bus. (In retrospect, I'd have to advise anyone running away from home to avoid public transport. It can play havoc with your nerves if you think that the person you are running away from is going to pass by the bus stop at any moment. Though to be fair to my mother, if she could have afforded it, we would have caught a taxi.)

We arrive at my nanny's, who opens the door with the weary distressed look we knew so well. She has a one-bedroom council flat, so we camp on her hire-purchase sofa and chairs, curled up like soggy animals.

My mother's brother, Paul, is called in to try to remedy the situation. Paul is thin and nervous. Nanny says he's extra sensitive. He talks and talks. My mother's crying.

The upshot of it all is that with nowhere to go, and no money, there's nothing to do but go back. Paul offers to drive us, which is a brave act, considering my father. But, when we get back home my father is still watching the telly, as if he hadn't even noticed we were gone.

There is a photograph of my parents from that time. My mother has her arms curled around her body protectively and she's smiling, but if you look carefully you can see the smile doesn't reach her eyes. You can see shadows there. I know that the cardigan and skirt she is wearing are second-hand, and the soles of her shoes are worn through.

You can see my father, he's wearing a well-cut woollen suit, an expensive-looking watch. He has a handkerchief folded neatly in his breast pocket. He's smiling and warily watching the camera at the same time.

You can see my sisters and me, lined up cross-legged. Bud frowns at the camera, Tigs eyes it as you would an intruder, Lu gleams her gorgeous smile, I look a bit ruffled, not unlike a buffalo surprised by a discarded apple core to the stomach. Bud's hair is tied up in a satin ribbon.

What you can't see is that we are starving, that there is no food. What you can't see is the freezing cold because the electricity has been cut off. What you can't see is that in every home but our home, the lights are on and Christmas is coming.

My father says to my mother, 'I've tried everythin'. It's your turn to do somefink.'

My mother looks away, as if his words have hurt her.

I know it's not a good time but I ask anyway, 'Can I have a new pair of shoes?' I don't want to go out in my old worn shoes any more. The other kids make fun of me. My mother takes my shoes and polishes them until they glow. She stuffs new paper in the holes, but you can tell they are broken shoes under the shine.

'They could all 'ave new shoes within the week,' says my father, looking at my mother.

She meets his eyes for a moment, then she starts to cry.

Bud clips me around the ear. I'm not quick enough off the mark.

'Look what you've done,' she says.

I go out feeling bad about my mummy crying and my shoes which still look funny. I try to hide my feet as I walk so no one can see, but there aren't that many low-lying bushes in our concrete jungle.

That night, we're put to bed early. I sit up. My sisters are asleep, but I'm awake and looking at the rain against the dark glass and how my breath fogs the glass. I practise a bit of writing on the glass. I draw a face. I hear our front door close.

I look out and see my mother and father all dressed up walking out to the van. This is a surprise. I look down at my mother, and even from my window I can tell by the way she holds herself that she is upset. Not happy, like you would think, to be going out.

The van takes a bit to get going and I can see rather than hear my father swearing at it. I watch the van disappear, a plume of smoke from the exhaust, the red tail-lights vanishing into the night. Where have they gone? I can't say why, but I feel uneasy.

I think maybe I should wake up Bud and tell her, but then I think she'd only get angry with me for waking her up and box my ears.

The landing light is on. I get up and go downstairs to make sure the front door is locked. The house at night has a different feeling, it's full of shadows and silence. I look in the kitchen, the blind is pulled down like a closed eye. I shiver. We are safe, aren't we? I go back up to bed and curl up in my blankets. I lie still, listening to every noise. I lie there for a long time, until I hear the rattle of the milkman starting his rounds. I fall asleep then.

When we get up in the morning there is food. It is a miracle. Rice Krispies, gold-top milk, big chunks of toast, and bacon frying in the pan. Bud, Tigs, Lu and I eat like there is no tomorrow. We eat until our stomachs hurt.

My mother is watching us with a small smile. My father looks at her.

'That wasn't so fuckin' 'ard, was it?'

My mother sits at the table, still in her dress-up clothes. I ask her if they've been to a party, but she tells me to be quiet.

'Your muvver's got an evenin' job so play quiet, she's restin'.'

Strangely, my father doesn't look happy about our prosperity, he looks angry.

I watch my mother go into the bathroom. I look at Bud. Bud *knows*.

'What's going on?' I ask.

'Mind your own beeswax, Kathy. You leave Mummy alone. She's tired.'

Bud takes a swipe at my ears and misses. I dodge past her into the hall.

My father yells at us, 'Shut up the lot of yer and git out to the playground.'

Bud lines us up. Ready or not. I take Lu and Tigs by the hand. We walk to the playground not stepping on any cracks in the pavement; if you do it's bad luck.

Every day a sign of our new-found prosperity pops up. My sisters and I pay a visit to the shoe shop in the high street. As if new shoes aren't enough, we are taken to Debenhams department store and bought new coats. Not duffle coats. Not anoraks. Proper coats with velvet collars. The kind you see rich girls in.

Lu looks at herself in the mirror for a long time. She runs her hand over the velvet collar, tosses her hair. 'Ooh la la.'

Mummy laughs and hugs us. 'My darling girls, you all look so beautiful.'

Tigs scowls. She'd rather be dead than look like a girl.

At home, my father views our new coats with approval. He looks at my mother.

'Now ain't that worth it? Seein' 'em?'

My mother gives him a look. 'I'm tired. I think I'll have a rest,' she says.

My father nods. 'I'll have a rest too ...'

'No,' says my mother, 'I have to sleep.'

My dad looks at her, getting angry. 'Suit yourself.'

'The money's there,' says my mother, turning to go up to bed.

My father helps himself from my mother's purse. He folds ten pound notes into his pocket. He slams the door, his new camel coat slung over his shoulders.

As soon as my father leaves the house, the atmosphere changes. We all breathe a sigh of relief. You always know if my father's in or out in our house; you can feel his presence in the pit of your stomach.

I creep up the stairs to have a look at my mother. She is asleep. I push open her bedroom door and watch her. She's curled up, one arm flung out, fist still curled as if even in her dreams she can't relax. You can see she's been crying, her mascara is smudged, like coal-tracks.

I want to curl up with her but Bud comes up behind me and closes the door.

'You leave Mummy alone!'

I dive out of the way before Bud can get a good box of my ears. I am too slow and catch a left hook which gives me a stinging sensation all the way back down the stairs.

I go outside instead.

Something is going on. I can feel it. No one is talking about it. Bud is my only source of information and whatever she knows she isn't telling. When I come back in Mummy is sitting at the table drinking a cup of tea and looking tired. She is dressed up in a new outfit.

'You look beautiful, Mummy,' says Bud.

'Do I?' Mummy looks at Bud.

Bud sits on my mother's knee and pats her. Mummy gives her a smile.

'I got you some biscuits for tea.'

Mummy puts big fat pieces of shortbread on a plate for us. I take one and put it in my mouth before anyone can change their mind. I suck the crumbly buttery finger and make short work of it. Lu nibbles hers delicately, Bud breaks hers in half, and Tigs puts hers in her pocket for later. I don't know what she's saving it for.

'How about tomorrow you all come with Nanny and me to the toyshop. You can pick out a Christmas present each. Whatever you like.'

My mother says this but I think I'm hearing things because what she's saying is *unheard of*. It's not that I'm suspicious, but there has to be a catch.

That night in bed, I hear my parents leave.

'What are you sitting up for?' Bud says, wide awake.

'Have they gone out?' I say, stating the obvious.

Tigs turns her football round. Lu rustles in her bed, then starts to cry a bit. 'I want Mummy.'

'None of you should be awake. Go to sleep,' orders Bud.

'We don't have to if we don't want to,' I say.

'I'm in charge,' says Bud, 'and if you don't go to sleep right now I'll ...' She thinks. '... Go to sleep, now, or there'll be no toyshop in the morning.'

We lie down immediately, like skittles. Grimnasty has spoken.

My mother emerges from her bed late in the morning, and at lunchtime we all catch the bus to the shops. Nanny has come as promised and holds our hands. Lu, Bud, Tigs and I pull our mother and Nanny along because we can't get there fast enough. We're feeling very merry and even Mummy, who is tired, seems to have cheered up.

All I know is that a few weeks ago we were looking in through the window without a penny to our name and now *we are inside the toyshop* with real money. I am too excited to speak. The narrow aisles are packed to the ceiling with every kind of toy in the whole wide world. I can smell the new-toy smell and see the bright cardboard packages. I look and look.

My nanny prods me.

'Go on Kathy dear, pick something.'

Pick something! I'm overwhelmed, I look around and my eye lands on a pink and lavender plastic pretend make-up set. It has a mirror, pretend lipstick, pretend eye shadow, pretend blusher, a pearly necklace and matching bracelet. I pick it up.

'Is that what you want, Kathy? Are you sure?' I nod, half expecting a slap at any minute and to be told, 'Put that down, you know we can't afford it.' Nothing happens. I look from my nanny to my mother, they're smiling. I stand there clutching my booty. Tigs, in her boy-like fashion, has selected a robot with flashing lights, Bud has picked an Etch A Sketch because she loves things she can control. Lu has picked a 'Ken and Barbie' doll set. Sheer American glamour. To my utmost astonishment, my mother leads us to the cash register and pays for everything. They are really to be ours it seems. Lu, Bud, Tigs and I exchange looks of extreme satisfaction.

We return home to our wonky kitchen table. Our toys are inspected by my father as my nanny takes out several dozen of her homemade mince pies.

'Nice,' says my father, smacking his lips and draining another cup of tea. 'You kids'll 'ave more room for your toys when we move.'

There had to be catch. I knew it.

'Don't look so worried. It's a classy gaff, not like the dumps round 'ere.'

With a sinking feeling, I imagine we'll be going back to the caravan site or worse, and believe me there have been worse.

My father says we've got the weekend to pack up. Lu, Tigs, Bud and I look at our mother for reassurance. 'It's all right,' she smiles, 'we're going to 16 Cumberland Road.'

That night, as I lie in bed, my lavender and pink make-up set tucked up with me, I hear my mother's voice over and over in my head, '16 Cumberland Road.' I've never heard of a Cumberland Road. I've only heard of Cumberland sausages. Maybe we're going to live next door to a sausage factory? I don't mind sausages, as long as I can have them with sauce.

Today, 16 Cumberland Road, Bromley doesn't exist. Developers have long since knocked it down. But back when I first saw it, it was unbelievable. I mean, to me, it was as grand as you could get. There was a curved drive and a huge fir tree growing in the front garden. The drive was gravel. I remember the crunch of it under my feet.

Even now, a gravel drive will take me back to my eight-year-old self standing on the drive with my sisters.

Crunch. Crunch. Crunch. I do some extra crunching, it's a good sound.

'Poor people never have gravel drives,' Lu informs me. 'Rich people have gravel drives.'

'Does that mean we are rich?' I ask her.

Lu sighs, giving me a pitying look because I'm slow on the uptake.

'Not really rich. If we were we'd have a swimming pool, wouldn't we?'

Tigs gives her football a good kick, it goes spinning over the gravel. Bud eyes up the fir tree.

'Hey, this is good for climbing!'

We scoot over to the tree and examine its potential. Sure enough, the perfect climbing tree. Long low branches and plenty of them. Mummy calls us.

'Girls! Come on!'

We scoot inside to explore. It turns out that this big old house is divided into flats, so we haven't got the whole place to ourselves. But who cares? Lu and Tigs and Bud and I run deliriously, incredulously, from room to room. My mother stands there smiling at us, even my father is smiling. We've got part of the garden to play in. We've even got our own garden shed! The shed is as big as our caravan used to be.

I test the waters of our new-found family happiness. 'Can we get a hamster?' To my utmost astonishment, I get a yes. I'm not exaggerating, but what with the toyshop incident and now this, I am giddy.

Lu, not slow on the uptake, narrows her hazel eyes and enquires: 'Can we can afford to go and see *Mary Poppins*?'

'Yes!' is the answer.

'Ruddy hell,' I think. 'Ruddy hell!'

A Respectable Family

Our new-found respectability has its price. We have come to the attention of the neighbours and hence the authorities.

'Mr Abbott?'

'Who wants 'im?'

My father is bent over Tigs' new bike. He is giving it a final touch of paint. The bike is red and white, Tigs gazes at it, like a boy in love. She hovers anxiously.

'There ya go. As good as new.'

Tigs collects her bike. My dad looks up, surprised that the visitor is still present. He wipes his hands.

'Yeah, love? What can I do for you?'

'I'm from the education department and we wondered why your children have not been enrolled in school.'

My father eyes up the lady visitor in her uncompromising knitted suit. She doesn't flinch from his green-eyed stare. You can tell she's dealt with tough customers before. He pauses, working out his best mode of attack.

'I don't believe in the education system as such.'

'That's all very well, Mr Abbott, but unless you particularly want the welfare authorities notified, it would be advisable to enrol your children … Highfield Junior, I believe, is your local junior school.'

'And what if I don't?'

'There will be consequences, Mr Abbott. Children need an education.'

There are some things that even my father can't avoid.

I feel a bit anxious about going to school. From what I've gathered, getting an education can be risky. I fervently hope that I don't encounter a 'bully' or any girls at all by the name of Belinda.

On Monday our father drops us off at our new school, and he doesn't hang around. We arrive in time for assembly, and before I know it we've been lined up in groups, our classes.

We are split up by age: Bud with the ten-year-olds, Tigs and me with the eights and Lu is with the six-year-olds.

To be honest, this whole school thing comes as a shock. Tigs and I find ourselves lined up with some of the beefiest kids I've ever seen. They have legs like giant bollards. I catch a glimpse of Bud, two rows ahead. She looks around at me and nods, her green eyes tense and alert. I can't see Lu, she's somewhere behind me with the little kids. I turn around to look but there's a boy the size of a lorry standing right behind me. He's got a face like a bag of chisels so I decide it's probably wiser if I don't catch his eye.

I'm big for my age, but still I have the distinct feeling I am in the land of the giants.

The only upside I can see is that opposite the assembly hall there is a school library with potential access to hundreds of books. This will make a change from sneaking out to the mobile library, whose literary selection has become somewhat wanting anyway – unless you're a particular fan of the most loathsome 'Chicken Licken the sky is falling' kind of book.

I make a mental note to enquire about the library the first chance I get.

At the end of assembly, the headmaster (from the size of his head you'd expect him to have a bigger body) makes a speech, welcoming us all. To my surprise he reads out the names of all the new pupils, including my sisters and me. I feel my face turning beetroot as everyone turns to examine us and I am deeply thankful that I am wearing my new shoes and not my old ones.

The first morning is a blur of impressions – the rows of desks, the smell of the toilets, the long echoey corridors and everywhere the stout pink calves of children bigger than me.

The morning break presents a major success. The girls turn their transistor radios on full blast. Not unnaturally, or because I haven't learnt any better, I start to dance. The music gets me inside so that I can't stand still.

To my astonishment my dancing is a triumph! I am unexpectedly the envy of the playground. This has not gone unnoticed by the hard nut contingent, who do not like 'Johnny come latelys' stealing their thunder.

A second triumph is waiting for me in the afternoon. All

the lonely years of reading everything and anything – the backs of shampoo bottles, cereal boxes, anything with words on it – have paid off!

I am sitting in the school corridor reading when the headmaster walks by. He eyes the book I am holding. It is not a regulation 'Janet and John' book ('Look, Janet look! Look, John look! …')

'What are you doing?' he asks.

'I'm reading, Sir.'

He snatches the book out of my hand and accuses me of lying. He has that look that grown-ups get when they think they've caught you out.

'All right,' he says, 'then read it to me out loud.'

I oblige. I recite in my best BBC radio voice, hardly dropping any aitches at all.

He marches off, taking my book with him, but the upshot is that I am given free access to the senior library on the condition I take out books approved by my teacher. At lunchtime, I run like the clappers to get to the library, so as not to waste a minute of book-browsing time. Oh, it is heaven. Row upon row of books, all just waiting for me!

On my way out, loaded with fresh literature, I am accosted by a hard nut. The hard nuts are not just poor kids, they are the offspring of the local criminal contingent. This contingent are mostly thieves, vandals and bullies. They are emphatically not respecters of library property.

'New girl!'

I look up and my heart sinks. The hard nuts are lined up around me, like the rocks of Stonehenge. 'You better come into the playground.' 'Not bloody likely,' I think, buying time and looking desperately about for a teacher. (Like policemen, rarely around at the time you need 'em.)

'What for?' I ask, which is really a superfluous question, because I can tell I'm what for. Tigs comes from behind them, with our lunch. She eyes off the 'Guard of Honour'. She stands beside me.

'D'you want your sandwich, Kathy?'

'Get lost, Sprout,' says the beefy sidekick.

The ring-leader is a weasly, spindly girl with crooked teeth. She looks like she's never had a decent meal in her life. But she looks vicious.

'You heard what she said, get lost!'

Not given to idle talk, Tigs puts her bag down. Her face is pale but her mouth has formed into a thin firm line. Only I know what that means. It's a gunfight at the OK Corral. Without warning Tigs headbuts the beefy sidekick with the full force of her bonce. A 'nutter' – a combat move that feels a bit like a concrete ball to the innards. This manoeuvre takes the beefy sidekick by surprise and, winded, she goes down like a wounded ogre. The other tough nuts blink in shock. They hesitate ... Reading this as weakness, I go at one of them, kicking her in the shins.

The commotion brings the teachers pouring out of the staff room. They like a fight as much as anybody. A bit of daily drama to break up the monotony. Soon we are separated, panting like children who have been in a fight. My library books are scattered on the dirty concrete, but Tigs and I exchange triumphant looks. The casualties are definitely on their side. The best form of defence is attack (that is, if you can't run away).

A teacher leads the 'bleeders' off to the nurse. I pick up my library books, and Tigs and I prepare for our telling off. All the while I think: what do you know? The hard nuts were soft nuts after all. After life with my dad, a bunch of sissy girls just ain't in the same football pitch. Bud and Lu turn up to escort us home. Bud's green eyes flash; she looks us over for signs of real injury.

'All right?' Tigs and I nod and we smile at each other, me with my bashed-up books and Tigs the acknowledged champion 'nutter' of the world.

Fresh from our victory we return home. To our disappointment, our mother is already at her evening job. We are alone. Bud, as usual, takes charge and leads us into the kitchen where Mummy has left out our dinner.

'Wash your hands or I'll box your ears,' says Grimnasty.

Plates of ham and coleslaw and packets of crisps are laid out for tea, and next to the plates are Picnic chocolate bars. One whole one each. (How quickly we've got used to all this richness!)

After tea, I dive out and hide in the garden shed, so there'll be no chance I'll have to share my Picnic with Bud. I eat the chocolate off the outside first, and save the toffee bits till last. (There's an art to eating a Picnic bar.)

I must have fallen asleep because when I wake up it's already dark. I feel cold and a bit scared. I open the shed door and see the lights from the house. How warm and comforting they look. I hurry up the path, but when I get to the back door it's locked. I bang and bang, but no one answers. I run up the side path, past the overhanging hedge – I can feel my breath coming in pants – and pelt up the gravel drive to the front door and press the bell.

It seems like a long time before my father comes. He opens the door and looks down at me. I can see from his eyes that I've made him angry, and I feel my stomach give an acid lurch.

'What time d'you fuckin' call this?' he says. I try to tell him that I fell asleep in the shed, but he cuts me off. 'You can fuckin' stay out and learn yer lesson. If yer stay out that's your look out and you can suffer the consequences.'

He slams the front door on me. I look through the misted glass and see his figure recede; that's when I realise he means it. Tears well up in my eyes.

After a while I hear the sound of the television and I know he's not coming back. I make my way back down the path to the shed, only now I am more afraid, and every shadow looks like a monster.

At that moment, I hear the back door open and Bud's voice calling, 'Kathy?' I run over to the back door. Her fierce eyes check me over to see how I'm faring. Of course, she daren't let me in but she furtively hands me a blanket and Lu's teddy, who's blue and, naturally, goes by the name of Bluebell.

'You'll be all right,' says Bud. 'Lock the latch on the shed.'

Only slightly comforted, I make my way back to the shed. I fasten the latch and lie down on some sacks, pulling the blanket over me. The sacks contain some sort of fertiliser which stinks, so in the end I sleep on some cardboard boxes.

Even when it's light, it seems like I still have to wait for hours before my father finally lets me in the house. 'Have you learnt yer lesson?' he asks, standing there in his pristine white underwear.

I nod.

'That's all right then,' he says.

If I didn't know better I'd say he was feeling a bit guilty for leaving his own flesh and blood outside all night.

We hardly see my mother at all any more. My father has two catch cries: 'You know your mummy is at work,' and 'Be quiet, your mother is sleeping.'

This Sunday though, my mother is home. She is in the kitchen overseeing a roast dinner. At the oven, she bends down to turn the meat over. My father sits at the table. She gives him a look. My father looks annoyed. He says, 'It's only a bit of meat, innit? It doesn't fucking count.'

They seem to be referring to something other than the dinner but I don't understand.

My mother starts to cry; my father gets up and tips our new table over. The plates, cutlery and glasses go everywhere.

Our old wonky table used to tilt on its own, but even a new one doesn't make things all right.

Like bullets, Tigs, Lu, Bud and I run to our mother. We cling to her hands, her legs. My father takes a lunge forward as if to hit us, but then he stops himself. He looks from us to our mother.

'Fuck it then.' He turns on his heels and storms out.

We wait to make sure he has gone. Then my mother bends down and sets the fallen table upright. We pick up the cutlery and plates and the broken bits and lay them on the table. My mother wipes her eyes and hugs us close. 'It's all right girls,' she says. 'It's all right.'

Jack the blind miner can see that it's not.

I suggest helpfully, 'Should we just have the pudding then and forget about the meat?'

The next week starts badly. The cat has gone to the toilet on the mat and someone has trodden the poo all over the house. My father, who is hygiene conscious, has gone mad. He lines us up.

'Lift up yer feet.'

Surprisingly, we all pass inspection, including my mother who is still dressed in her going-out clothes from the night before.

Bud, who is astonishingly brave for her age, narrows her eyes and says to my father, 'What about your feet?'

My father hesitates, looks at Bud and then looks at his own feet, shod in rather nice new burgundy slippers. Sure enough there's a telltale smear of cat poo on the underside.

'Fuckin' stinkin' bloody thing. You wait till I catch it. I'll wring its fuckin' neck.' He hops towards the toilet and I try to find our crappy cat to warn it to lie low for a while. I sincerely hope it really does have nine lives, because it will need them.

*

On the outside things are definitely better – we have food, new clothes, toys, a school. On the inside they are worse. The atmosphere seems to be getting more tense by the day. There is an undercurrent. My father has begun watching my mother like a cat.

Sometimes my nanny comes over to look after us when my mother has left for work. One such afternoon my father waltzes in with a new pair of glasses.

'What d'ya fink, old girl?' he addresses my nanny cheerfully. 'These are the latest. Celebrities wear these. The rich and famous.'

Nanny looks at my father. 'Ted,' she says, 'where is all this going to end?'

'I don't know what you mean,' he says.

Nanny looks angry. Now, my nanny seldom gets angry, so when she raises her voice, well ... it means something.

I stop scoffing her homemade scones and concentrate on what they are saying.

'You do know what I mean,' she says. 'It has got to stop. My daughter is getting sick.'

My father glances quickly at Nanny and then avoids her eyes. 'Now don't go getting all worked up. Everyone is happy. The kids are happy ... look at them.'

Nanny doesn't take her eyes off my father. 'Marie is not happy.'

'Tell you what,' says my father. 'Tell you what, seeing as yer so concerned, how's about I take 'er on a holiday. That's it! A holiday? We could all do with a break.'

*

A holiday it is. We are spending the week in Bournemouth. This is *high* excitement for Tigs, Lu, Bud and me because we have never, never actually been on a proper holiday before. Mummy has bought new suitcases for the trip.

We are booked into a bed and breakfast on the seafront. Lu, Tigs, Bud and I have our own room with two single beds and two camp beds. There's a sink in the corner of the room and a little table with doilies on it and miniature soap. The bedspreads are a bit of a disappointment to Lu as they are orange nylon.

As I always say, nothing good can come of the colour orange. 'Common,' says Lu, 'dead common.'

Tigs takes her football out of her suitcase. She had quite a lot of trouble squeezing it in and now it bounces up and down on her knees. If she was a boy she'd probably play football.

My case weighs a ton because I packed too many books and Bud made me carry her Spiky doll.

Bud's Spiky doll is an extension of Bud really, she makes you sleep with it and seeing as the doll's made of hard plastic, its feet and hands spike you in the bed. Invariably Spiky doll is consigned to the floor during the night. Bud regularly rescues her doll and points accusatory fingers at us. As I said, remarkably alike really.

Bud has claimed the best bed by the window. I've got the other proper bed because I am big, and Tigs and Lu have the camp beds. It's quite cosy. Now all we need to do is wait for the rain to stop.

Shiny new buckets and spades have been purchased, along

with large pink sticks of Bournemouth rock. The letters B O U R N E M O U T H go all the way through to the end.

My father and mother dump us at the beach. They are dressed up nicely, in new seaside holiday clothes. My mother picks her way awkwardly over the sand, she doesn't want to ruin her new sandals.

'Now shut your cakeholes and point your ears towards me.' Obediently we look at our father.

'Now stay put here and don't go wanderin' off. Don't go near the water. Yer mother and I are goin' for some fish an' chips. Bud, you're in charge!'

My father folds his arm through my mother's and leads her off. She looks back uncertainly at us. We don't say anything as it is impossible to answer with a stick of rock in your gob.

As time goes by we edge nearer the water. Sand has only so much charm and what harm is there in a tiny little paddle? We all run into the ocean. What a thrill! The water is so icy cold it makes us scream.

'Don't go in deep,' admonishes Bud. Which is good advice because none of us can swim.

I wade thigh deep into the waves. The water is green and full of seaweed. I look down, and in the murky depths I see my limbs moving. I am transported: the sky, the water, the taste of salt.

Suddenly Bud is pulling at me. Shouting. It takes me a bit to understand. Lu has disappeared.

Bud, Tigs and I scan the horizon, the beach, the water. Lu is nowhere to be seen.

Bud flings her head back and screams, 'LUUUUUUU!'

Over the brim of the sand I see my parents running down the beach, my father just ahead. He's pulling off his jacket and running like the clappers. He doesn't stop at the water's edge but wades straight in, trousers and all. He reaches down and pulls Lu from the waves. She is limp. He rolls her onto the sand and massages her chest. Lu starts to cough, she spews up seawater and starts to cry. My mother falls to the sand and clutches Lu in her arms.

My father gets up and turns to Bud.

'What did I fuckin' tell you? Don't go near the water! You were fuckin' in charge and look what you did!'

Bud can barely gasp for breath. My dad grabs hold of her and shakes her. Bud starts to sob. My father in his fury picks up Bud's new spade and snaps it in two. My mother starts to cry then. 'Ted, she's only a child,' she says.

My father picks Bud up and flings her away from him. 'Get away. Get away yer selfish stupid little bitch.'

Bud is crying uncontrollably. She didn't mean it. We didn't mean it. My mother picks up the broken spade. She looks at us, helpless.

Maybe it was the holiday that was the last straw. I don't know. But the following week we come home from school and my father is standing there with a funny expression on his face.

'Yer muvver's up and left yer,' he says.

Bud, Lu, Tigs and I look at each other, speechless.

'She's fuckin' gorn,' he says.

At first we can't believe this is true, but after a while we see that he is serious. It's not the idea that Mummy has left that is so hard to believe, after all she's tried it before. It's just that this time she hasn't taken us with her.

This is a catastrophe. Where has my mother gone? It's a mystery. She surely can't have abandoned us and yet the evidence seems to suggests otherwise, the facts comprising: 1) absence of mother, 2) missing clothes and personal items, 3) extremely angry father.

To avoid the fallout from our father, Bud herds us into our bedroom. Tigs' face has pinched up, she looks anxious. Lu's eyes are filled with tears, her long eyelashes sticking together. Bud musters her not inconsiderable faculties and glares at us defiantly.

'Mummy will come back. She's just working on a plan.'

'What plan?' I ask.

'I don't know,' admits Bud. 'I know she would never leave us.'

We nod, but the problem remains. A hard indigestible pain, somewhere in the vicinity of our hearts. We agree to remain on the alert and to keep an eye on each other. This makes a pleasant change as usually we don't agree about anything. (Bud is still very much the amateur pugilist. I am sure that my hearing is being affected but that is the least of my problems.)

To assist with the situation I make a 'Lost' poster of our mother. I'm pleased with the likeness I draw, despite the hole in the paper where I rubbed too hard with my rubber. For good measure I decorate all around the edges with love-hearts.

Encouraged by my sisters, I venture out of the bedroom

and give the poster to my father, suggesting we put it up at the police station.

My father doesn't like the idea at all. He, of course, has a very low opinion of the constabulary. For instance you'd never catch him watching *Dixon of Dock Green* on the telly. He's much more your Alf Garnett man.

'Kathy, come 'ere,' my father says.

Naturally I cringe, I think I'm for it. But he takes me in his arms and gives me a cuddle.

I remember that hug. I remember that hug like it was yesterday. I remember the smell of my father's clean skin, the Brylcreem in his hair. I was as high as a kite over it.

Still, the poster idea doesn't happen. My father puts real advertisements in the paper instead. No one knows where my mother has gone. The days drag on. We have things like cold chips for breakfast because all my father can think about is my mother. I wear my school shirt inside out because it looks a bit cleaner that way.

My father has taken to continually checking the letterbox and picking up the telephone. He's not sleeping at night. I hear him pacing up and down until dawn. Everything is falling apart.

Proof of this is that when I ask my father about lunch money, he hands over a pound note. A whole pound! After a brief skirmish with Bud, she commandeers the cash. Still, I wonder how many Walnut Whips, Sherbet Dabs, Liquorice Imps, Curly Wurlys, Flying Saucers and Milk Bottles you can get for a pound.

We wait outside the school for my father to pick us up in

the van. It's already getting dark and the streetlights make the wet pavement shiny. We wait at the bus shelter to stay out of the rain. We wonder, as we have wondered every night, if our mother will be home when we get back. We don't say anything but that's what we hope.

Tigs has thrown up at the kerb from eating too many peppermints. She ate so many she was rattling. The only good thing you can say about peppermints is they're cheap. You can get more peppermints for your money than anything else.

I've got a bag of Flying Saucers, coloured rice paper filled with sherbet. Lu only got a tube of Love Hearts, sweet, chalky disks of delight – with the bonus of messages about your love life. However, I can't prove it, but I know Bud swindled us over that pound.

My father rolls up in the van. You can tell by the way he's driving that there's been no sign of our mother. He swerves up next to the pavement nearly running over our toes. We hop in and he drives off at breakneck speed. We clatter round in the back of the van like skittles. I eye Tigs for a while, because you can never tell with her when she's going to blow.

(On our holiday, for instance, we were sitting down to dinner and my father was carrying on, 'Is it fresh, your catch of the day? 'Cos if it's last Sunday's catch of the day, you'll know it. It is? Right, then, fish and chips all round.'

Tigs was sitting there, a bit quieter and paler than usual, which I can tell you is *very* pale and quiet. The waiter brought the food. I looked at Tigs and was about to say, 'Are you all right?' when she promptly threw up straight into her plate. She did it very quietly so no one noticed except me and Lu and Bud. We kids all looked at each other. The adults didn't notice. My mother told us to eat our food up. Pretty soon the waiter returned to take our plates away, including Tigs', which was full of vomit. 'They didn't like the fish?' the waiter asked my parents. 'Shall I get them something else?' 'Nah,' said Father. 'If they won't eat they can go without.')

But, we make it back home without mishap, which is a relief.

When we pull up at our house, Nanny is waiting outside with her Tesco carrier bags. My father is pleased to see her, thinking that maybe she has news from our mother. ''Ave you heard from 'er?' he asks.

Nanny looks at him, dead level. 'No, have you?'

My father shakes his head angrily.

'What do you think she's playin' at?' He starts striding up and down the drive like a Hitler.

After some time of his ranting and raving Nanny says, 'Don't you think we should go in? The children are getting cold.'

My father calms down and looks at us a bit surprised, as if he'd just noticed us all standing there mottled with the damp and frost. He opens the front door sheepishly.

'I've brought you over some dinner,' Nanny says.

She has two casseroles, with new potatoes and an apple pie. She would've lugged them over on the bus. Makes you feel sorry for the people on the bus, smelling our dinner but not being able to have any.

However, before we can eat we have to hunt around for money for the gas meter. Soon the rooms are warm and cosy.

You can tell my father is comforted by Nanny's presence, though he'd never admit it in a million years.

After dinner Nanny tucks us up in bed.

'Nanny?' I say, looking at the outline of her fluffy grey head. 'Is Mummy coming back?'

'Now Kathy, don't go worrying. She's got good reasons for going and four good reasons for coming back.' She kisses me on the top of my head. 'Night-night.'

Nanny goes downstairs, I hear her at the front door saying goodnight to my father. After looking after us she has to catch two buses home. I'm glad I'm warm in bed and not outside in the cold and the dark.

I can hear by their breathing that Lu and Tigs are already asleep. Tigs snores and Lu rustles about her bed like my hamster.

I can't stop thinking about my mother. What has happened? Maybe she's gone to one of her brothers, my uncles? You can see their wives' faces turn ashen when my mother turns up on their doorstep. Usually they do everything they can to avoid having her (and us) stay. I imagine the thought passes through their minds that they'd be stuck with us forever. Usually they give my mother some money, enough to make her go away but not enough to make any difference. They adhere strictly to the 'You've-made-your-own-bed-and-now-you-must-lie-in-it' school of thought.

Maybe they've had a change of heart?

The thing I just can't understand is why my mother

wouldn't have taken us with her. I'm worried. I whisper to Bud, 'You awake?'

'Yes,' she says. I can tell she's worrying too.

'Do you think Mummy is all right?' I ask.

'I dunno.'

Then I say what's been lurking in the back of my mind since my mother went. 'You don't think she's been murdered?'

Bud sits up then. I can see her eyes. The fear makes everything stop. Makes every detail vivid. In my imagination the question hangs in the air already dripping with blood. Like the title on a Hammer House of Horror film.

Bud tells me to shut my trap.

Lost and Found

I daren't voice any further fears about my mother's safety. I can see that my father is going to the dogs. He has stopped shaving. For that matter, we are all going into a decline. Even my hamster seems to be off his food. We play our *Jungle Book* record but the joy has gone out of it.

One evening we are sitting in the lounge in front of the telly when our father bursts into tears. Great heaving sobs. At first I think it's got something to do with Cilla Black, who is on the telly and who is enough to make anyone cry, but then I see he's not watching the telly at all.

It occurs to me that things must be very bad because I have never seen my father cry like this, not even over the piana. These are real heavy tears.

Bud, Tigs, Lu and I look at each other astonished. Bud gets up and gives my father a tentative cuddle. Then we all do.

He says, 'At least I've got you gurls, that's one thing.'

I'd go so far as to say that if my father had a normal heart it would be breaking. But Nanny say's he has the heart of a stone, and you can't break that, can you?

My father's friend Tommy and his wife Alice come round because it's a fine to-do that we have been abandoned. Alice makes us all tea.

'Come on Ted, snap out of it,' Tommy says.

My father goes off with Tommy to the dogs.

Tommy and Alice were around when my mother met my father. To hear Alice tell it, you would think she was talking about different people. She says it was summertime. She says it was in the days when Londoners would go hop-picking in Kent. Alice says my mother and father were inseparable. That they all used to make fun of them because they were so lovey-dovey.

I try to see my parents in my mind, when they were young and carefree. Slim and tanned with the radiance of the sun still warm on their skins. I can see them at the end of the day, sitting in a pub garden somewhere. Drinking long, cool shandies and waving away the midges flying above their heads. I can hear their laughter and I can see them searching for each other's hands because they are in love. Sometimes I close my eyes and see them sitting in that hop garden in Kent. I put them in one of those glass things that you shake up. Only instead of the snow, I have sunlight and midges and newly mown grass. And love, of course. Love would be in the air, like sparkles.

We've known Alice since we were little. She used to sleep with Tigs and me when we were babies and my mother's hands were full. With Alice, you get the feeling that she's sensitive and that she should never have hooked up with a man like Tommy, who is a bit like my father. In fact my father and Tommy go back a long way. 'They're of the same ilk,' my nanny would say, not nicely.

News flash! When my father and Tommy get back, Alice is excited. My mother has telephoned! She is going to telephone again at four o'clock. It seems hard to believe. Bud nudges me. 'Told you so.'

With the matter partially resolved, Alice and Tommy leave us. 'There! Didn't we tell yer it would sort itself awt?'

My father perks up no end. He tells us to get cracking and to tidy everything up. Bud does the dishes, Tigs and I do the beds and Lu picks up all the clothes. My father does a bit of vacuuming and then rushes into the bathroom to spruce up.

He's in there for an hour at least. After he comes out, he smells of shaving soap and his hair is slicked back with Brylcreem.

We are ordered into the bathroom too, to brush our hair and wash our faces. It's almost as if our mother is coming for an inspection, that she could take one look at us and decide we're too scruffy and she won't want to stay. Bud flattens her curls with water, Lu combs out her hair carefully and fixes her headband. I plait my straight hair and Tigs doesn't even look in the mirror. As a concession to the event she wipes a bit of dirt off her shoes by rubbing them on the back of her trousers.

On the dot of four the phone rings. My father picks up the receiver. We listen, he listens. Then he says, 'I don't care what you do, Marie, believe me, just come 'ome.' Then he says, 'Where are you?' They have a short talk and my father puts down the phone like she's hung up on him. You can tell he's upset.

We wait for him to tell us what's going on, but then he jumps up suddenly, like he's got an idea of where Mummy is, and hurries us all outside and into the van.

We get into the van as we are, coatless, there isn't time. Even before we've sat down properly my father swerves up the drive and has his foot down on the pedal.

Bud, Tigs, Lu and I all exchange looks, we know better than to say anything when our father's worked up. We hold on to each other, sliding one way then the other. I can see out of the window that we're heading into town. Maybe our mother is waiting somewhere?

Just as abruptly as we started, we stop. Our father parks on a yellow line and tells us, 'Stay 'ere a minute.'

We watch him stride off up the street. 'Do you think he's gone to get Mummy?' I ask. Bud gives me a withering look like I'm the last in a long line of idiots. I take that as a good sign.

Lu snuggles up to me. 'I'm cold,' she says. Tigs, who even in our hurry has managed to grab her football, gives it a few turns in lieu of comment. We wait.

The windows begin to steam up with our breath. I wipe off the condensation to look out and nearly jump out of my skin because a traffic warden is peering in. Her nose-tip is pressed to the window like a snail's body.

Bud climbs into the front and winds down the window. The traffic warden starts to say we'd better move on, before noticing Bud's a kid. Bud tells her, 'My daddy had to find a toilet, he's very sick since he came back from the war.' It's the same old story we've been using for years. The traffic warden looks at us suspiciously. 'He'll be back in a minute,' says Bud, giving one of her best smiles. The traffic warden softens, 'He shouldn't be leaving you kids alone.'

At that point our father turns up. He's about to launch into the story when the traffic warden makes the mistake of saying, 'You shouldn't be leaving children unattended in a vehicle.' Our father pulls himself up, eyes blazing with anger. 'D'you want to repeat that?' he says. 'Nobody tells me 'ow to look after my kids. Not unless they fancy picking up their teeth with broken fingers.'

The traffic warden looks a tad wary. 'I'm going to have to give you a ticket.'

Our father leans right in close to her face, and opens his mouth. He bares his teeth and gnashes them at her. You can almost feel his hot breath on your own collar.

'You wouldn't like me to get upset would you? I get upset when I get upset.'

The traffic warden takes a step back, disinclined to chance it.

Our father leaps into the van and takes off, nearly running the traffic warden down. (I don't think she had time to note the registration number, and even if she did, she'd have found that our numberplates are conveniently muddied over on a permanent basis.)

The ride home is like the ride out, fast and erratic. Sliding around in the back, we keep our mouths shut.

When we get home, my father sits by the telephone all

evening. He keeps looking at it, hoping it will ring. But it doesn't. He forgets about us, about dinner, so Bud gives us all a bowl of cereal.

At bedtime when we go to the toilet, my father is sitting in there with his trousers down, not moving.

'Isn't Mummy coming home?' Bud asks.

Our father looks at us numbly, like we're not even there.

Bud shoos us out up to bed. She says to our father, 'Daddy, remember you've got us.' But it's like he doesn't even hear her.

In the morning the phone rings again. It's Mummy! There seems to be some negotiating going on. There's a series of phone calls with each one of our parents hanging up on the other. Finally, I hear my father swear, 'Look, you've had yer say. What do you fuckin' want?' He listens and then he nods. Bud and Tigs, Lu and I are all listening hard.

When he hangs up the phone, his face has completely changed. He smiles at us. 'There,' he says, 'didn't I tell yer yer muvver would come 'ome?'

Despite the urgent and burning desire of my sisters and me to see our mother, our father takes us to school. He dumps us at the gate and swerves off down the road, barely missing several of our schoolmates on the zebra crossing.

The lessons drag on interminably. Subjects I usually like are as boring as hell. Every now and then, I peer around at Tigs who has her pencil clamped in her hands and a look of quiet desperation on her face. Mind you, the minute she enters the classroom, she gets a bit of a trapped look. The only two subjects that make her happy are art (and she's painstaking) and sport. Tigs has perfected her 'teacher avoidance' strategies ... Of course, she's not always successful, and inevitably teacher contact comes her way. When this happens Tigs' face turns scarlet, and she casts around for some sort of escape; there being none, she resigns herself, like a creature caught in the headlamps of an oncoming express.

Today, more than usual, every single task is an obstacle in the way of the end-of-school bell.

On the dot of four o'clock I am out the door ahead of the rest of the stampeding children. Like a racehorse out of the gate, flying past noticeboards that read: 'Strictly No Running in the Corridor.'

Father is waiting in the van, engine running so you can tell he's keen to get off. We jump in and look at his face to gauge if Mummy is home or not. We set off at breakneck speed and arrive within seconds, it seems, at our front door.

Lo and behold, our mother is standing in the lounge room with two suitcases. 'How did you get here?' asks Bud.

'By minicab,' she says.

She might as well have said 'magic carpet' for it seems just as miraculous. She looks all tanned and dressed up, like a stranger. Our father and mother look at each other. He nods, she nods. They don't say anything.

Our mother scoops me and Tigs and Lu and Bud up in her arms and hugs us. There are tears in her eyes and she looks us all over very closely to check that we are okay, to see if there are any marks of suffering on us.

I can't speak for the others, but I show my mother the

warts which have sprung up all over my thumbs. I can see that she is impressed by their size and number.

Mummy's brought back treasure. Things I have never seen before. Soap in red and black boxes wrapped up in black tissue paper; paper fans and mother-of-pearl combs. She says they're from a country called Spain.

To celebrate, our father takes us all out to a caf for tea. We girls eat our chips quickly, lest an argument break out and we have to leave in a hurry. Old habits die hard, and a chip in the mouth is worth two on the plate.

The atmosphere is tense. I can see my father is bursting to speak, but my mother looks at him and says, 'Not now. When the children have gone to bed.' I'm totally astonished that my father doesn't argue. He just drinks his tea and looks at my mother as if she might vanish.

He keeps looking at the gold bracelet she is wearing on her wrist. I surmise that it is Spanish gold.

'Were you kidnapped by pirates?'

'Not now, Kathy, I'm tired. We'll talk about it tomorrow.'

Bud, Tigs, Lu and I are packed off to bed sharpish, which is a good thing because with all the emotional upheaval we're knackered.

After extra pleading, our mother relents and, in spite of my father, sits on our beds and tells us a story. We're curled around her like bear cubs; Tigs has hold of one hand, Bud the other, and Lu and I rest our heads in her lap. I fall asleep listening to her voice and smelling her smell and I'm happy.

I dream it is summertime and I am running through the long grass with my sisters. We are all out of breath, it is warm and lovely. When we flop down in the grass I look over to a stream and see my parents wading into the water. Mummy has her dress tucked up, and Daddy has his trousers rolled up. They are catching tadpoles for us. We are a happy family in my dreams.

It is my mother's scream that wakes me up. Bud and I sit up at the same time. We are dead frightened. After the scream there is the sound of a slamming door. For a moment we are paralysed with fear.

Then Bud says, 'Get up Kathy, or we'll be sitting ducks.'

I leap up and put on my coat; Tigs is up, silently clutching her ball. Lu is still fast asleep, it takes some rousing her as she can sleep through anything. She complains bitterly as we help her with her coat.

Together we creep out of the bedroom to see what's going on. To our amazement the flat is empty. We go outside. I take Teddy Bluebell along because he doesn't like being left out.

It's freezing. The cold hits your body like a number 57 bus.

At first we can't see anything, but then we realise that the neighbours' lights are blazing.

Our father is outside their flat shouting through the letterbox. 'Come out Marie, I know yer in there. Just tell me, where did the bracelet come from?'

The neighbours won't let him in. He's getting more and more furious. From experience we know it's best to make ourselves scarce, so we hide in the fir tree that grows beside the drive.

My father puts his fist straight through the glass panel in the neighbours' front door. He doesn't even notice that he has cut himself. That's when I realise that the situation is now very serious. My eyes are drawn to the blood dripping off his hand, like syrup. He reaches in through the hole and undoes the lock. We hear a man's voice and then Mummy screaming.

'Get out the fuckin' way and you won't get hurt. I want my wife.'

There's a sharp crack and then a yell.

'Right, you've asked for it.'

I can see Bud looking through the needles. I can see her breath in the air. Panting. I can see Tigs' pale hands clutching her football. I can see the big tears forming in Lu's jewelled eyes. We don't move. It's like we are frozen in the tree.

A blue light cuts across the darkness. The sirens get louder, ascending like screams. A police panda car swerves up the drive, sending bits of gravel spinning into the night. Policemen, walkie-talkies crackling, climb out of the car and hurry up the steps to the neighbours' flat. They disappear inside.

Off in the distance another siren approaches. An ambulance pulls up and blocks our view of the flat.

We can hear different footsteps crunching on the gravel, people talking in low tones.

Bud looks at me, and by unspoken agreement we all climb out of the tree together. When we get to the ground we peep around the ambulance to see what's going on. My heart is thumping because I'm sure my parents have killed each other. But all we can see is the neighbour being helped out with a bloody bandage around his arm.

As we try to get closer a policeman stops us.

''Ello, 'ello,' he says, 'what's this?'

Bud does the talking.

The policeman speaks into his walkie-talkie. 'PC Hobbs. The domestic in Cumberland Road. There's four kids. No … four of the little blighters … *girls.*'

He says the 'girls' part as if we're some strange type of animal. Like the pushmi-pullyu in *Doctor Dolittle.* Then he listens for a bit. 'Wilco, Sarge,' he says.

'Righto, girls,' he turns to us. 'D'you fancy a ride in a big police car?'

He leads us to his car, and actually I am quite interested because I've never been in a police car. But Bud pushes past him and tries to run into the neighbours' flat.

'Oi!' the policeman yells, and chases after her.

Bud makes it to the front door but she runs straight into another policeman. He carries her kicking to the car. 'Now be a good girl,' he says to her. 'You've got to look after your sisters.'

Bud looks at us, all sitting quiet as mice in the back seat. Then she looks back at the door of the flat as if making up her mind. Without another word she gets into the car with us. The policeman locks the doors and drives off. I'm not sure, but I think we have been arrested.

Never Trust a Social Worker

I was disappointed to learn that PC Dixon was not at the station and that the station wasn't Dock Green.

Real life is nothing like what you see on telly.

My sisters and I were parked in an office with fluorescent lights and not in a gaol cell at all.

Tigs turns her football around. 'Do you think my bike will be okay?'

'Yeah. It's in the garage, isn't it?'

Tigs nods.

Getting arrested isn't very exciting. You just sit around for hours. The only good thing is that we are given cups of fizzy drink and Golden Wonder crisps.

'Where's Mummy?' Bud asks.

'Don't worry, everything is all right,' a police officer tells us.

Which isn't true, otherwise what are we all sitting in a police station in the middle of the night for?

'Are you going to lock us up then?'

A policeman pats Bud on the head. 'I don't think we lock up little girls yet.'

After much to-ing and fro-ing via the telephone, a social worker is called in.

'Here are the girls,' says the sergeant.

'All I need in the middle of the night,' she replies. 'Aren't there any relatives?'

'There's three uncles apparently. But no one will take them in.' The sergeant shakes his head, 'And they say blood is thicker than water.'

The social worker looks at us. 'I'm Mrs Darling.' She wears blue eye shadow like the Avon lady.

'We're all staying together, my sisters and me,' Bud says.

'Of course you are,' says Mrs Darling. 'Come on out to the car.'

We follow Mrs Darling. 'There's not enough room for you all, so Lu will have to go with the nice police lady.'

We don't like the idea of Lu going in a different car. Bud hesitates, she's older so she knows.

Mrs Darling sees her hesitate. 'Everything is all right Bud. Come on, get in before you catch cold.' Bud, Tigs and I get into the back seat of her car.

Mrs Darling drives us to a tower block of flats. We go up the concrete stairs and there's a lady waiting for us with her front door open. The lady says, 'About time. I've been waitin' up half the night.'

Mrs Darling introduces us. 'This is Bud and Tigs and Kathy.'

The lady tells us her name is Margery. 'Yer all need a good night's sleep, I should think.'

'Well that's that then. Goodnight.'

'Hang on a minute. What about Lu? Where is she?' Bud glares at Mrs Darling.

'Lu has gone to a nice foster home, temporarily, of course …'

'You said we were all staying together,' accuses Bud. Mrs Darling looks a bit ashamed, like she's played us a nasty trick. Which she has. Bud doesn't give up, won't give up. Her eyes blaze with a fury that matches our father's.

'We won't stay. We won't stay without her.'

But Mrs Darling doesn't care and the Margery character locks the front door.

'You'll do as you're told!'

When you're a child you are at the mercy of any old grown-up, good or bad. Bud knows this and she falls silent. We all fall silent.

I take stock. 1) We don't know what's happened to our parents. 2) Lu has been taken away. 3) What will happen to my hamster and goldfish if I'm not there to feed them? (Will they die?)

Margery makes us sit in her kitchen; she smells of cigarettes.

'Take that football off the table for starters.'

Margery spoons out tinned macaroni cheese. Bud doesn't eat it in protest, and Tigs doesn't eat it because she doesn't like macaroni cheese. I would like to eat mine but as I put a spoonful to my mouth, Bud looks at me like I'm betraying her. So the upshot is none of us have anything to eat.

'Suit yerselves. I suppose it's all been a bit upsettin'.'

Margery leads us to a bedroom down the hall. It has two

bunk beds and a fold-up bed crammed against the wall. It is a boy's room. Tigs is impressed by the pictures of George Best on the wall and the kit model aeroplane hanging from the ceiling.

'There yer go. Tuck yerselves in. Goodnight.'

Margery turns off the light and closes the door firmly. I can't swear to it, but did I hear a key turn in the lock? Bud reaches out and takes my hand in the dark.

'All right?'

We all lie in the same bed holding hands and fall asleep, still with our coats on, too exhausted to undress.

In the morning, alas, the situation is not all just a bad dream – Margery appears in a nylon housecoat with sweat stains under the armpits. 'Rise and shine. Ready for some breakfast?'

In the kitchen Margery gives us last night's macaroni cheese on toast. It hasn't improved upon further acquaintance. I look across at Bud who nods at me. The three of us attempt to eat the sludge.

Margery comes back in. 'Are you good girls or naughty girls?'

We're not sure where this line of questioning is leading, so we nod.

'I just have to dash out for a while, in the meantime I'd like you to do a job for me. You can clean the silver.'

We're not sure what Margery's talking about. We watch as she spreads newspaper all over the table and lays out silver cutlery. Then she gets out a tin of polish and shows us how she wants her cutlery cleaned. We do it the way she shows us, and it's quite fascinating to see the dull metal come up all gleaming.

'I want it all done by the time I return,' says Margery. 'On no account answer the door or the telephone.' And off she goes.

Bud, Tigs and I are relieved. At least she's left us alone, albeit locked in. We have a good snoop round.

The flat has two bedrooms, the boy's room we slept in and another bedroom which is obviously Margery's. Hers is all in satin with love-heart cushions. This is a surprise because to look at Margery you'd never think she was the type. Margery's bed looks as though it belongs to an altogether different creature.

The rest of the flat consists of a lounge with a sofa and pouffe in green plastic. A telly is parked in the corner with a bowl of goldfish on top. There's a novelty cigarette lighter in the shape of a bowl of fruit on a coffee table. We play with the lighter for a bit.

'We better stop before the gas runs too low,' Bud says. We put the lighter down. The toilet is next to the bathroom with a sliding door. The toilet flush is one of those new button ones and we all have a go flushing it.

After a while we go back to the kitchen and finish polishing the silver, because we don't need to get into any more trouble.

As we are sitting there, we come up with a plan.

We decide to butter Margery up so that she will tell us where our parents and Lu are and what's going on.

'Then what will we do?' I ask.

'Then we'll run away,' Bud declares matter-of-factly. 'The first chance we get. When I say go we just go!'

There's silence for a bit while Tigs and I digest this. I have to admit it seems like an incredibly daring plan. I imagine that we will be like the Famous Five and we'll go and live on Kirrin Island with a dog called Timmy and drink lashings and lashings of ginger beer (whatever that is; I imagine it's like Tizer, only better).

Even after we've cleaned the silver Margery isn't back. As part of our 'butter-up-Margery' plan, Bud decides that we should do the washing-up and vacuum the flat. This should please Margery no end.

I'm given the job of vacuuming, only it isn't vacuuming because Margery has only got a carpet-sweeper. It keeps jamming up with all the fag ends. Margery obviously smokes a lot, there are fags ends stubbed out everywhere, even floating in the fish tank.

What with our father's exacting hygiene standards we're pretty good cleaners.

When Margery arrives home she looks at us in astonishment. 'What are you doing?'

'We thought we'd clean up a bit seeing as you had to go out,' says Bud, diplomatically.

'Well I never. In all my born days.' But I think she's impressed, especially as her silver lies gleaming on the table.

'Well girls,' she says. 'Why don't we have some lunch and then I'll take you to the park.'

Margery serves up macaroni cheese again. She's obviously got a job lot of the stuff, probably off the back of a lorry. I exchange looks with Bud.

'Mmmm,' says Bud with feigned pleasure, and starts eating.

We follow suit and eat up the macaroni cheese. Although, to be accurate, you wouldn't say Tigs ate hers as much as divided it up on her plate. Sauce one side, macaroni the other. I silently swear by Almighty God that if I ever make it to adulthood I will never touch macaroni cheese ever again.

'That was nice wasn't it?' Margery says. 'You can have an ice-cream in the park since you've all been so good.' Bud nudges me because our plan seems to be going well.

The park is one of those big ones with a wrought-iron fence all the way round. It has a duck pond and a bandstand. The bandstand smells of urine, but Margery doesn't seem to mind. She sits down and lights up a cigarette.

'My feet are killing me. I'll just have a rest here for a bit. Why don't you go and look at the ducks?'

As we head for the pond Margery calls after us, 'Stay where I can see you.'

'Stay where I can see you,' is one of those odd adult instructions. How do we know where she can see us and where she can't? As soon as Margery is out of sight, we crouch down in the hedge to have a talk.

But before we start Tigs decides she needs to go to the toilet. But she would never dare go alone.

'Wait here,' orders Bud as she takes Tigs by the hand and marches her towards the ladies.

To kill time I start looking along the hedges to see if there are any birds' nests or better still, birds' nests with eggs in them. As I'm looking I come across a man standing ever so still in a duffle coat.

'Hullo,' he says.

'Hullo,' I say.

'What are you doing?' he asks

I tell him about the birds' nests.

'You must like animals.' He smiles at me, and looks over his shoulder like he's checking for something. 'Would you like to see my mouse?'

'A mouse?' I say, curious.

'Yes, my mouse.' He has his hands in front of his trousers and I can see him holding something. I lean in to have a look.

'It's an odd-looking mouse isn't it?' the man smiles at me. 'He hasn't grown any hair yet.'

The mouse is pink and smooth with a peculiar mouth at the end. It's the funniest looking mouse I've ever seen.

'Where's its ears and its tail?' I ask.

'They haven't grown yet.'

'Can I hold it?' I look up at him, and the suggestion seems to make him happy.

'You can't hold him,' the man shakes his head. 'He's a bit of a shy mouse. But you can stroke him.'

I reach over to stroke the mouse, and the strangest thing happens. The mouse gets bigger. The man tells me it's a magic mouse, that if you give it affection it grows bigger.

'Would you like to come home with me?' says the man. 'I've got all sorts of other animals at home.'

'What sort of animals?' I watch fascinated as the mouse

gets bigger and bigger. More like a big fat sausage than a mouse.

'Uh … oh cats … and dogs … and … um …' The man seems to be having trouble breathing, and the mouse starts squirming about.

'Giraffes? I've never seen a giraffe close up.'

'Oh … yes … ah … I have a pet giraffe,' gasps the man. The mouse suddenly looks like it's being sick, white stuff spouts from its mouth.

Right at that moment, Margery comes round the bushes with Tigs and Bud. They're carrying ice-creams. Margery takes one look at me and the man and screams. She drops her ice-cream and the man in the duffle coat runs off in a panic. Margery rushes over.

'Oh you poor girl. What did he do to you?' She hugs me.

'He was showing me his mouse,' I answer truthfully, nonplussed by the surplus emotion.

The kerfuffle has brought some bystanders over. The grown-ups all look serious, as if something terrible has happened.

One lady volunteers to go off and find a copper. Tigs and Bud stand around sympathetically but equally puzzled. Soon a policeman arrives. He's been running and his face is red from the exertion. Margery tells him that there's been a man exposing himself and 'God knows what else.'

The policeman crouches down to talk to me. I tell him all about the mouse, but when I come to the stroking part he looks aghast. 'What's the world coming to?' He shakes his head and writes everything down in his notebook. The policeman takes all the details and a full description of the man in the duffle coat. 'One duffle coat – black,' he writes.

He assures Margery that he's going to have a good look around the park. Then he looks down at me.

'Didn't your mother ever tell you never to talk to strangers?' he asks.

To be honest I can't remember if she did or didn't. All I can think of is that my ice-cream is melting on the path and I probably won't get another one.

'Let's go home,' says Margery. 'That's given me a nasty turn.'

'What about Kathy's ice-cream?' pipes in Bud. Sometimes I really love my big sister for being so pushy.

'We'll get you another on the way home,' says Margery, and for the first time I think that maybe she isn't that bad, because a lot of grown-ups would have said no outright.

As we walk home, Bud tries to get information out of Margery about what's happened to our parents, but Margery doesn't seem to know.

'Can we see Lu to make sure she's okay?' Bud asks.

Margery flashes her a not unsympathetic look. 'There's nothing I can do today but I'll ask your case workers and see what they say.'

When we get back to the flat, Margery tells us to play quietly while she has a lie down. Apparently the incident in the park has worn her out.

Bud, Tigs and I have more important things to think about, like what to do. In the back of our minds we're thinking that every hour that goes by something terrible could be happening to Lu.

Bud suggests that if we try to find our way home maybe Mummy would be there to help us rescue Lu.

We resolve that if no information has turned up by tomorrow we'll run away.

I say to Bud, 'We're just like the Three Musketeers.' Bud says, 'The what?' I say, 'You know, like, all for one and one for all!' Bud, not unexpectedly, tells me to shut my cakehole.

Wards of the State

The morning of the day we are going to run away dawns. We haven't decided at precisely what point we will make a dash for it but, as I said to Bud, it's only common sense to wait until after breakfast. Which, surprise surprise, turns out to be another tin of macaroni cheese.

After breakfast, just as we're eyeing the door, Margery informs us that a car is coming to collect us.

'Are we going home?' demands Bud. But all Margery will say is, 'Hurry up and get ready.'

We haven't got much to 'get ready', only our coats. Tigs has her football, of course. I'm looking around for Bluebell. I ask Margery if she's seen him and she laughs. 'That horrible old thing. I threw it away, it had moths.' I am dumbstruck. How could anyone throw a teddy away? Tigs offers me her football to hold. I look at Tigs. She's a funny stick, she never complains and she always understands.

Silently we troop out to wait for the car. Sure enough, a Humber pulls up and who should be sitting in it but the traitorous Mrs Darling. To our utmost relief Lu is sitting in the front seat waving through the car window. Never have I been so happy to see someone in my life. She's wearing a new pink dress with dots on it, and has shiny washed hair. It seems Mrs Darling is able to fit us all together in the same car after all.

'Hullooo. It's me,' Lu says, opening her door.

We fall on top of her in a kind of group hug, until Mrs Darling tells us to get in the car.

'Home?' asks Bud, eyeing Mrs Darling suspiciously.

Mrs Darling smiles. 'Come on, you're all together and we'd better get going. It's a long drive.'

We get in, trusting that we'll be taken home.

Margery reaches in and gives us all a hug. I can't be sure, but I think she's upset. For a second I feel a bit sorry for her standing there in her nylons with her swollen feet.

As we drive along, Lu fills us in on what happened to her. She was taken to a big house in the country. She shows us a new Tiny Tears, and I must admit I'm a bit jealous because I would've liked a new doll too.

Lu is one of those people who are born lucky. She's the sort of person who, if she drops her toast, it will always land butter side up. Misfortune may rear its head but Lu always lands on her feet. You can't blame her. Some people are born under a lucky star, that's all.

The four of us are chatting away in the car, feeling happier, when Bud asks if we are there yet. Mrs Darling doesn't answer at once. The way she hesitates makes us realise something's wrong. 'Nearly,' she says finally.

A little later, she pulls up outside a big grey government

building. Then she turns around to us and says brightly, 'Here we are then girls, out you get.'

'This isn't home,' accuses Bud.

'Now, now, young lady,' says Mrs Darling. 'Let's not get our knickers in a twist.' She drags Bud out of the car, and we follow.

It turns out we're at the child welfare department. But, as we tumble into the waiting room, who is sitting there but our father! He stands up and we nearly knock him down again in our enthusiasm.

'Where's Mummy?' we ask at once.

It's only been a few days since we've seen him, but our father looks thinner and older, like he's been ill. Bud grabs his hand. 'Are we going home, Daddy?' she asks.

He avoids the question. 'D'you fancy a walk in the park?'

He takes us to the park, we walk around and after that we walk about the streets looking in the shop windows. It's been raining, and as it begins to get dark you can see all the lights reflected in the pavement. We're starting to get cold so our father takes us to a caf. He says we can have anything we want. This is a turn-up for the books so, in spite of the cold, we order Knickerbocker Glory ice-creams, except Daddy who just has his usual cup of tea with several sugars in it.

'Where'd they put you?' my father pumps us for information. We tell him, then he looks sad, shaking his head. 'I can't believe it. I can't believe she'd give yer up.'

This perplexes us. 'What does that mean?' asks Bud.

'That means yer muvver has given you to the guvverment as wards.'

'I don't wanna be a ward,' says Bud.

'It's not up to me,' our father answers grimly.

Pressing him for further details, we learn our mother has run away with her 'paramour' and doesn't want us around.

'What's a paramour?' I ask.

'It's 'er new fancy man,' he replies.

'But doesn't she love us?'

My father turns and looks at me and his eyes fill up. 'No. She doesn't.'

This takes the wind out of our sails. We are all silent as we try to understand this unimaginable fact. Bud looks from my father to Lu and Tigs and me.

'I'll look after you,' she says. 'I'll look after them, Daddy.'

He looks at Bud, 'That's me Bud,' he says. 'Don't forget.'

Bud nods.

By the time we come out of the caf the rain has started up again.

'We better get you back,' my father says.

Lu starts to cry.

'For God's sake. I promised I'd bring yer back, diden I?'

Lu quietens, because she doesn't dare do otherwise. We take it in turn to hug him goodbye.

When we get to the big grey building, Mrs Darling is waiting. Our father asks her if he can see us again. 'What about tomorrow afternoon?'

Mrs Darling says she doesn't see why not.

'See you tomorrow,' he says. We wave at him through the back window of the car as we're driven away. He stands on the pavement in the rain, watching us go.

I keep looking back. My father's shape recedes into the distance. A black smudge, a smear against the rain. I turn my head and look out the front window.

Where are we going? We pass down streets I don't recognise. The day has now faded and the dark closed in. I look at the lights of the houses, each one looking cosy and inviting. After a while the houses thin out and we pass from the city lights to no lights at all. There's nothing to see out the window except the dark outlines of trees pressing in on the road.

It seems like a long time before Mrs Darling slows the car down and we turn into a long straight lane lined with hedges. The car sweeps up a drive and we stop in front of the formidable silhouette of a huge house. We get out of the car, hugging our coats round our bodies. We jump up and down to keep warm.

'Here we are. Pilgrim House,' Mrs Darling informs us.

I look up at the light which illuminates a big black and white front door.

Mrs Darling rings the bell. 'It's a children's home,' she says.

Pilgrim House

The words 'children's home' strike terror in my child's heart.
I reach out and prod Bud in the back. 'Run for it. Come
on!' I yell at her. Bud turns and looks at me, she doesn't
seem to understand my alarm. I want to run, but I can't
without my sisters.

Mrs Darling grabs me. 'Whatever is the matter?'

'I've read all about children's homes,' I'm telling Bud, Lu
and Tigs. 'It's like when they take a horse to the knackers
and make it into glue.'

Bud looks from me to Mrs Darling.

Mrs Darling tightens her grip on me. 'Don't be so ridiculous. This is a perfectly lovely home.'

The front door opens, light falls from the doorway, and
a tall shadow commands the darkness. 'Ah, the Abbott children. We've been expecting you.'

Mrs Darling pushes us into the hall. We freeze like
animals caught in headlights. I know that my sisters and I
are done for. They are going to kill us. I want to cry but the
tears are frozen lumps in my throat.

We look up to see a tall, thin woman looking down on us. 'I am the superintendent. You will address me at all times as Superintendent.'

Mrs Darling makes a rapid getaway. She pulls up the collar of her coat against the cold and bids us a traitorous goodbye. 'Now be good girls,' are her parting words.

'Bugger you,' I think. 'Bugger you.'

The superintendent-person leads us down a long red-and-black-tiled corridor. All the while I'm looking for an exit. We turn up a wide staircase, along another shorter corridor and stop outside a darkened room.

'Here we are. We don't want to wake the other children do we? Get into bed and we'll sort you out in the morning.'

She leads us on tiptoe into a dormitory. I make out the shapes of other sleeping children. We stand uncertainly by the door and all look at each other, not sure if this dormitory business is a trick.

'Come on children, we can't stand about all night. Pop into bed. I've put you near each other.'

Tigs places her football on her bed. The superintendent looks at it as if she's about to take it away.

'It's clean,' says Tigs, going slightly red in the face.

The superintendent looks at Tigs and then at her football.

'Shhh. All right then. On no account wake the other children. Goodnight.'

The superintendent leaves the room, taking her nightlight with her. The minute she has disappeared several heads pop up from their pillows.

'Hullo,' says a girl from the next bed.

'Are you new?' inquires a voice from across the room.

'Got any sweets?' asks another.

'Is this a real children's home or is it a glue factory?' I ask.

'It's a real children's home all right,' a girl answers.

The superintendent has crept back ever so quietly, and she suddenly bellows, 'NO TALKING! IF I HEAR ANOTHER WORD OUT OF ANY OF YOU, YOU HAVE MY WORD, THERE'LL BE NO FATHER CHRISTMAS!'

Like magic, everyone disappears under their covers and is immediately quiet. My sisters and I climb into bed. All of a sudden I'm feeling very, very tired.

'Tigs? You okay?'

Tigs nods to indicate that she is.

I lie down on the pillow and smell the strange new bedclothes. All the events of the day crowd into my head. I look over at the windows. I can't see any stars, only the shadows of trees, falling on the window like bars.

The next morning, we are put straight about every issue by the other children. 'Saturday is for walks and cleaning your shoes,' 'Sunday we get cracklin'' and, finally, 'Our parents are dead, are yours?'

I reply loftily to this. 'We are only here temporarily as our parents are coming to get us.'

One girl snickers. I don't like the sound of her snicker. I draw myself up to my full height. 'What's so funny?' I demand.

'Nothing.' She turns away.

There's a dark-skinned boy near me. He whispers, 'That's what everyone says when they first get here. It's better not to get your hopes up.'

'Are your parents dead then?' I ask.

'Dunno,' he shrugs.

'How long have you been here?'

'Since I was three.'

I look at him closely. He has to be nine or ten years old. I take in his creamy dark skin, his long brown eyelashes and his funny fuzzy hair. In all my life I've never seen such a beautiful boy. I wonder how anyone could not love him. Of course, I don't say this.

'I'm Louis Browne,' he says, smiling at me. His teeth are perfect and white like a Colgate 'ring of confidence' ad. I smile back.

'Our mum went straight through the windscreen and broke her neck,' I am informed by twin boys called Ronald and Donald.

I look at these two boys and wonder at them. They are what you would call natural redheads, covered in freckles and topped off with bristly hair, which has been unsuccessfully controlled with dabs of Brylcreem. They have higgledy-piggledy teeth. If you ask me, when God made Ronald and Donald, he had only one colouring pencil on him and unfortunately it was orange.

Ronald and Donald are thrilled to have another set of twins in the home.

Even though Tigs and I are not identical, being twins gives you a slightly higher status in the Kingdom of

Children. At first though, no one believes we really are twins because we don't look anything alike. Next, they don't believe that Bud and Lu are our sisters, as Bud looks like my dad and Lu looks like no one because she is so beautiful. Of course, they have to believe we are related after a while because it's a fact, plus we've all got the same surname, haven't we?

The superintendent turns up at this point. 'Come along – we want to get your clothes sorted out.'

'Are we going to the back-of-the-lorry shop then?' Bud asks.

The superintendent raises an eyebrow and leads us down another corridor to a room that is jam-packed with outfits.

'This is Mrs Wood who looks after all the clothes and laundry,' she says. 'You're to do what she tells you.'

We turn to inspect Mrs Wood, who is herself giving us the once over. Mrs Wood has curly black hair and a mole growing on her cheek. I watch, fascinated, for a while, as it wobbles when she speaks. I don't think I'd like a mole like that and if I had one I'd cut it off or decorate it with something to distract attention from it. Maybe sequins?

'Well lovies,' Mrs Wood's mole is saying, 'how's about some smashin' new clothes?'

Being girls, we're not averse to new clothes, but to our dismay she pulls out four frocks all in the same dull pattern. Tigs looks desperate because she hates dresses of any kind. 'Have you got any trousers?' she asks.

'We'll get to those,' says Mrs Wood, and then she makes a joke: 'You can have any colour you like so long as it's brown.' Hilarious. I don't like brown at all, but Bud says I have the worst taste because brown is very 'in'.

After some time measuring and fitting, Mrs Wood sends us off.

''Um 'ack 'ater for your crows,' she says, her mouth full of pins. She sends us in the direction of the bathroom armed with brand-new tins of pink Gibbs toothpaste, new toothbrushes and red flannels.

After our encounter with the cavernous bathroom we rattle about the enormous house like odd buttons in a tin. The cold is withering. We find a radiator and huddle around it, but even the radiator is tepid.

The superintendent comes by and tells us we'll catch chilblains and why don't we get some fresh air? She herds us outside, an implacable shepherd. Then she closes the hefty black and white front door firmly. Even if you could reach to ring the bell to get back in you wouldn't dare.

Once outside there is nothing for it but to explore. I wander off and am amazed to discover that Pilgrim House is in the country. Or what I presume is the country. All around are open fields. Because it is winter the land has the cold flinty look of an angry man with a pursed mouth. Everything seems furrowed up, closed, waiting for the spring.

A black crow caws at me from a leafless tree. I can't make up my mind whether he's warning me off or just recognising a fellow inhabitant. My tummy rumbles.

Out of the corner of my eye I see that my sisters have discovered a playground with a swing and a roundabout. I run over to those familiar bobbly shapes in the frigid landscape.

By lunchtime we are blue with cold when finally the door is opened. We run inside like chastened house pets.

We follow our noses to the dining room, led by what we soon recognise to be the unmistakable and faintly repulsive smell of institutional cooked food.

The children pouring into the dining room are those too young to be off at school.

Bud, Lu, Tigs and I sit down at the spare places.

I overhear the dinner ladies talking. 'What? All four?'

'Where's the parents? Dead?'

'Oh no, I heard they just don't want them.'

'Crying shame.'

It dawns on me that they're talking about me and my sisters. I suddenly realise that we're stuck here. The thought makes my heart sink to an all-time low.

'What's the matter with you?' Bud pokes me.

'Why are we in here?'

'Mummy will get us out,' Bud says.

'Yes, she will,' agrees Tigs.

Lu replies, with her practical mind, 'Mummy is the one that put us in.'

I now realise what it was I heard, or rather felt, when I walked into Pilgrim House. A vibration in the air. A plaintive lament. The sound of a hundred desperate hearts. The hearts of lost children all beating out the same tattoo: love me, love me, love me, love me, love me. Each lost child hopes down the years – though they fear that there is no hope – that sometime, somewhere, somehow, someone will love them.

The desperate sound of unloved hearts is overwhelming. I quickly concern myself with the very serious business of food.

I am trying to get Tigs to swap her chips for my peas. If there's one thing Tigs likes, apart from peppermints, it's peas. (Lu on the other hand would rather die than let a pea pass her lips. I once read her the story of 'The Princess and the Pea' and she declared that she too was a princess, which I guess accounts for her aversion.)

Tigs hands over half her chips, and I give her, generously, the whole of my peas. For dessert I am disappointed with the watery rice pudding. There is no strawberry jam on it. I ask about jam but I'm told that it is locked up. Apparently all condiments are locked up as a precaution, presumably against us helping ourselves.

After lunch it transpires that we're to collect our new clothes and put them away in our lockers. There is a locker by each bed, with the child's name on it. I can see where they've rubbed out someone else's name and put mine over the top. No one can tell me what happened to my predecessor.

We have new labels on our clothes, printed neatly. I look at my new address. *Katherine Abbott, c/o Pilgrim House, Pilgrim's Way, Nr Westerham, Kent.* Black and white proof that I am now considered an orphan.

By the time I've tidied up my new clothes, the other children begin coming in from school. We're to do homework – or should that be children's-home work?

The plump lady who is in charge waddles around the room. 'Call me Mrs Stanley,' she tells us. 'You can just do some drawing if you haven't got any homework.'

Mrs Stanley gives my sisters and me a brand new box of colouring pencils each. I like a bit of drawing and I set to with a will. There is nothing more pleasing than a clean page to draw on, and the pointy tip of a sharp new pencil. You can smell the newness of them both.

I am particularly careful to write my name on my new possessions, because I don't want anyone nicking them.

Before long it's bedtime. There's a choice of warm milk or Bovril. I choose the Bovril because I don't like milk.

Adults, if you haven't noticed, are forever chucking milk down your neck. I'd rather eat swede and that's saying something, because if there's one thing that makes me vomit it's swede (mashed or cubed).

I traipse off to our dormitory with my sisters and all the other kids.

As much as you can ignore them in the day, at night your heart's desires come crowding in on you. Alone in your bed all that you keep secret comes and lies down with you. As I push my toes into the icier reaches of the bed, I wish that my mummy was there to tuck me in.

'Goodnight,' I call out.

To my surprise, the other children all echo 'goodnight' back. Which goes to show that we're all probably thinking along the same lines.

Sawdust in Our Tea

It is 1970. The new decade opens unremarked at Pilgrim House. For us though, Mrs Stanley has got a message. 'Hurry up girls, you've got a visitor.'

Visitors are kept segregated and out of sight, lest it upset the children who don't get any. Secrecy is supposed to be maintained by all parties. Some chance.

There is no doubt in our minds that our mother has come. Due to the inclement weather our visit takes place in the sports shed, hidden from the main building by a dense hedge. This visitors' hut is accessed by rickety wooden steps. There is damp carpet, an inhospitable gloom and absolute chill. It might be said that a visitor would stay longer but for the physical discomfort.

We scamper up the steps like squirrels expecting nuts. There, standing in the semi-dark, is our mother. Mummy. She's wearing a white scarf over her long dark hair, and a leopard-skin fur coat. She looks like a film star.

We hurtle our bodies into hers and wrap our arms around her legs, clinging like monkeys.

Mummy has brought us all sweets. She says it's best we eat them right away.

I disengage my teeth from a large golden humbug to ask, 'Are we going home?'

Mummy looks at the damp-stained carpet as if she doesn't want to answer the question. Then she sighs and gathers us together, holds our hands and explains, 'It's very difficult right now, but I am sorting everything out. You will all come home again as soon as I can manage it. I love my babies.'

I digest this news, which isn't good news, but it's better than staying here forever, like Louis.

'What about Daddy?'

There's a silence. My mother looks at us and her face hardens. 'I don't want you talking about Daddy any more. He's not any good and we're all going to start a happy life without him. Okay?'

We nod.

'I don't want you writing to him or anything like that. It will only upset everything. You want to come home with me, don't you?'

We nod. I think guiltily of the letter that I've just written. Perhaps if I had known it was my last letter I might have said something else, or at the very least checked the spelling.

Dear Daddy,
I hope you are well and I hope that pussy is all rite and I hope my gold fish is all rite to and if you see Nanny

*please tell her that if my hamster has babies do not touch
them or her mother will eat them.*

*There is a round-about and some swings and a swim-
ming pool and ther is a big garden and it is on a farm
and there are corn fields and I am aloud to play in them,
so now I must say good bye for now.*

With all my love KATHY
XXXXXXXXXXXXX

To escape the gloom and the awkward subject of our father,
we go for a walk. We take turns holding our mother's hand
because there are four of us and only one of her.

Too soon, it is time to say goodbye. She hugs each one of
us and says, 'Goodbye, my babies.'

We watch her walk up the drive and into a waiting taxi.
We smile and wave. 'Bye, Mummmeeee.'

The taxi pulls away, and we stand in the field, hands still
sticky, feeling sick from eating too many sweets, and from
homesickness.

Poor Louis comes up; I've saved him a single humbug.
He's so pleased that I wish I'd been less greedy and saved
him more.

'What did you do on your visit?' he asked.

'Oh, we just talked a bit and ate sweets.'

Louis nods his head gravely. 'Did you hold hands?'

'Yeah. We held hands a bit in turns and then it was time
to go.'

'Did you get a hug?'

'Yes.'

'Did you get a kiss?'

'Yes.'

'Your mum must love you then, eh?'

'Yes, Louis.'

Louis looks so sad that I truly wish he had a mother to love him. I don't know what to say, so I give him a hug. 'That's direct from my mother to you.'

I make up my mind to ask my mother if she'll adopt Louis, and then we can have our own brother and he can have a mother too.

Around about this time, with the winter drawing in, we start at a new school in Westerham. Oddly, for a school located in the country, it has a concrete playground.

My sisters and I line up at the first assembly. Grey school uniforms, grey skies. Dreary and cheerless. The headmistress sits down to play the piano, a thunderously righteous hymn. The woman's name is Mrs Gudunov, pronounced 'good-enough'.

She introduces my sisters and me: 'This term we have some new pupils who I want you to give special considera-tion to, they are poor unfortunates from Pilgrim House ...'

The whole of the rest of the school turns to eye us in our Pilgrim House clothes.

Mrs Gudunov has done us no favours. Being a 'poor unfortunate' from Pilgrim's means that you are a prime target for bullying. The other kids know there are no parents around to stick up for you.

By morning break I have learnt the Pilgrim House anthem. It goes like this:

There is a rotten dump
Down Pilgrim's Way
Where we get bashed about ten times a day
Egg and bacon we don't see
We get sawdust in our tea
That's why we're gradually
Fading away …

The Pilgrim House kids all stick together in the playground. Safety in numbers. We play kids' games, hopscotch and skipping, all the time keeping a wary eye on the other children, who are waiting for their chance.

Their chance comes. One of the boys takes Tigs' football away from her. He's a big boy, bigger than me, but I don't care. I couldn't give a shit. 'Bugger you,' I think. I follow the boy to the other side of the playground, through enemy lines. The other kids pull back and let me walk through, watching me carefully. I walk up to the boy.

'Can you give me my sister's ball back, please?'

The boy sneers at me. He bounces the ball up and down on his knee like he owns it.

I can't help myself, I feel my father's temper rising up in my veins. I feel my father in me, I feel his body in my body.

'Give me the ball back.'

'Nah. Wotcha gunna do about it?'

With nothing to lose, nothing, I hurl myself at the boy.

I can't 'nutter' like Tigs but I use every muscle, every bone, every single piece of my being to fight him. I feel as strong as a fully grown person. I am not afraid, not in the least bit. I have made up my mind to kill him. From far away, I can hear the boy screaming piteously. I don't stop. I carry on kicking, scratching, biting, hitting. The well of anger in me is too deep. It is an inexhaustible supply.

A teacher prises us apart. It takes me some time to focus on what's happened, on what she is saying. Everyone is looking at me in a shocked kind of way. Everyone has gone quiet. I look across at the boy. His face is bleeding, he's crying and his snot mingles in with his blood.

'What on earth's got into you?' the teacher says as she shakes me.

I don't answer her. I twist out of her grasp and bend to pick up Tigs' ball. I wipe the blood off it and hand it to my sister. Tigs takes the ball. I can tell she's embarrassed because everyone is looking at us.

The teacher takes the boy and me inside. The boy is taken off to first aid and I'm told to wait outside the head-mistress's office.

Mrs Gudunov inspects me.

'Kathy, isn't it?'

I nod.

'That's quite a temper you have there. If you don't watch it that temper will get you into serious trouble.'

I don't say anything. I look at the patterns on the carpet which are interesting grey swirls that look like comets.

'Young ladies do not fight, don't you know that? It is

most unbecoming and unfeminine. No one will want to marry you!'

I say nothing. I stare at the carpet.

'Kathy, are you sorry for hitting that boy? Kathy? Look at me.'

I look up, our eyes meet. I don't know what she sees in my eyes, but it's not remorse.

'Are you sorry? Kathy?'

She waits for me to answer. I can't find the words to explain. The silence grows. It grows and grows like a prize pumpkin at a fair.

'What do you have to say for yourself?'

She waits. For once I can't find anything to say. I feel somewhere inside me a kind of shame, but also a kind of joy.

'Very well. I have no alternative but to report you to the superintendent at Pilgrim House. Hardly an auspicious start to your first day here, is it?'

Not-good-enough-Mrs-Gudunov sends me back to the classroom. When I walk in silence falls. The teacher stops writing on the board and all the other children watch me as I go to my desk.

I look across at Tigs and can see she has her ball under her chair. In that moment I realise that although I am in disgrace, the other children will never try to take the ball from Tigs again.

Back at Pilgrim House, Bud greets me with one of those looks that only disapproving big sisters can give.

Immediately I'm called to the superintendent's office.

All the kids know what's happened so they gather to watch me go in.

First thing I notice as the door closes behind me is that the superintendent has a proper tea set laid out on a tray with cake and sandwiches. For one optimistic moment, I think I've been invited in for a tea party. My mouth fills with saliva and I can almost taste the strawberry cream on my tongue. But it is not to be.

From the look on the superintendent's face, I know she isn't going to share. She begins to lecture me on the evils of violence, all the while scoffing one treat after another, occasionally spitting crumbs out at me by accident. I wonder how she stays so thin, considering the amount she eats.

'What have you got to say for yourself, Kathy?'

I say nothing.

'Your behaviour this afternoon was lamentable. You are going to have to learn how to behave in society. You can't go around hitting people willy-nilly.'

Still I say nothing.

'Kathy? Take that sullen look off your face. Are you listening to me? There is absolutely no excuse for your uncontrolled outburst ...'

I'm wondering how long this game is going to go on, probably to the last jam tart. I am also wondering what kind of punishment is going to be dished out. The other kids have filled my imagination with all sorts of horrific tales. Maybe I'll be whipped or put in stocks. While I'm thinking, the superintendent stops talking and looks at me as if she's making up her mind.

'Seeing as you're new, I'm going to give you the benefit of the doubt on this occasion. What am I going to give you?'

'The benefit of the doubt,' I reply, doubtfully, scarcely able to believe my luck.

'But if there is ever, *ever* a repetition of today's incident, then the punishment will be swift and severe. What will the punishment be?'

'Swift and severe.'

'Swift and severe, *Superintendent.*'

'Swift and severe, Superintendent.'

'Now off you go Kathy and don't let it happen again.'

I leave the room as quickly as I can, lest she change her mind.

Outside her office, Tigs, Lu, Bud, Louis and the other kids greet me. They have been hovering to see whether I come out alive or, if it had gone the other way, to witness my screams of pain.

'Are you all right?' Bud asks, appraising me keenly. I nod.

Satisfied, Bud slaps me on the back and skips off to play.

By the day's end, I've wound myself up and exaggerated the whole story of how I nearly killed a boy. Mrs Stanley tells me to settle down and do my homework before bed.

'That's enough excitement for one day, Kathy,' she says. 'You should be ashamed.'

That night, as I'm falling asleep, Louis whispers across, 'Are you asleep?' And I say, 'No.'

I hop out of bed and slip into Louis' bed. It's unexpectedly warm. I feel a bit embarrassed, and I think Louis does too. He puts his arms around me and I put my head on his chest like I've seen grown-ups do. We cuddle awkwardly. Neither of us really knows what else to do. So after a while, because there's not much room, we agree I should get back into my own bed.

'But Kathy,' Louis says as he sits up, and I can see the shape of his fuzzy hair outlined in the dark. 'When we get big, will we get married?'

'Yes, Louis,' I say. I see his white teeth flash and I can tell he is smiling. I am smiling too. Vaguely I wonder if you can marry your own brother, but I'll worry about that later.

Day in and day out through the winter, my escape from this place is in books. I tuck myself away in a corner and read and read. Sometimes when I look up, I am surprised to find I am still here.

Yes, I had grown used to Pilgrim House. Was it a bad place? Not particularly. A good place? Not particularly. It was a place that served up the necessities and nothing extra. There were too many of us for extras. Besides, we were the poor, and the poor should be grateful for everything they are given.

As so often happened if I was found in my corner, I am torn from my reading and told to go outside into the bloody ruddy 'fresh air'!

Bud has been put in charge of organising games – what a surprise! Aside from being the bossiest person you've ever met, she never stops for breath. She has you playing games you don't like, piggy-in-the-middle, for instance. (Guess who's never in the middle?)

Sick of the game's injustices, I go to sit on the round-about and sulk.

Bud starts to scream at me. At first, I don't pay any attention because she's nearly always yelling at me to do something or other, but then I notice all the other kids screaming as well and running helter-skelter towards the house. I look around to see what the commotion is and see a man climbing through the hedge. I start to run, too.

Then I hear Bud scream, 'It's Daddy!'

I was in such a state with the massed hysteria that it could have been the Loch Ness monster after us. I didn't stop running until I was inside.

Once I'd calmed a bit, I couldn't help thinking that I didn't even recognise my own father. In less than a year he had become the stranger, the enemy.

Bud comes in later, her eyes looking red as if she's been crying. Tigs, Lu and I are waiting for her.

'Did you speak to him?'

'Yes,' Bud says. 'He says they won't let him see us any more.'

I nod. Tigs bites her lips and Lu sucks on a strand of her hair.

'He said didn't I remember him? Didn't I love him? He said would I give him a cuddle?'

'Did you?' I ask.

'Yes,' says Bud. 'Then the police came and he had to go.'

The three of us are silent. We all feel the same: confused and pretty crappy. We had run away from our own father.

The Season of Goodwill

After the father incident, I fall sick. Chickenpox, nothing unusual. I am put in isolation and allowed no visitors, not even my sisters. The vanquishing blow, however, is that I have nothing to read. Nothing. I have nothing to get better for, so I stay sick. After several weeks the superintendent pays me a visit.

'Now, Kathy, we can't have you malingering in here forever. You wouldn't want to miss Christmas, would you?'

Christmas? I'd forgotten about Christmas. Like a spotlight it appears on my horizon. I start to get better. Eventually, I am allowed up. I am allowed to mingle with my fellow inmates.

Bud appraises me keenly and jabs me in the upper arm. 'All right?'

I nod, scratching at the last of my poxy scabs.

Tigs regards me seriously. 'I've saved you some mints.' She hands me several lint-covered peppermints that have obviously spent a year or so in her pockets.

'Thanks,' I say.

Lu smiles and gives me a cuddle. 'Hullo Kathy. Better?'
I nod.

Ronald and Donald fill us in on Christmas.

'Statistically, you've got a higher chance of being adopted at Christmas than at any other time,' says Donald.

'Yeah,' says Ronald, and for a moment I see a flash of hope beam across their faces.

'Apart from that,' Louis says, 'Christmas is, you know, like the season of goodwill and all that. So all the people feel dead sorry for us so you know we're in high demand.'

Louis is right. To my utmost astonishment every day brings another do-gooder to our doorstep. It is a giddy social whirl.

One well-wisher says, 'The poor wee creatures, fancy having no family at Christmas. Let's give them all a visit to the pantomime.'

So, my fellow inmates and I are bustled into the velveteen interior of a theatre. We sit in the stalls, admiring the red padded seats and the hooded lighting.

Even though it's a matinee, the air smells of a mixture of cigarette and cigar smoke, perfume, and make-up. Grown-up smells, all rolled up into a package of intense anticipation. The heavy red curtains part and the magic begins.

'Ladies and gentlemen, boys and girls. Welcome to the panto.'

We are encouraged to BOO like hell when the Ugly Sisters make their appearance, and we do so with gusto. Oh, how great is the theatre! All the characters coming alive right out of the book – Cinderella, Prince Charming, the

Fairy Godmother. At the play's end we all clap and clap and
the actors look quite pleased with us (we do make up the
majority of the audience).

Despite desperate pleading, Mrs Stanley will not let us go
backstage; we are due, she says, at a special Christmas party.
She herds us out of the theatre to the waiting coach. I look
back regretfully.

'I could live in a theatre,' I whisper to Lu.

'I could live in a palace with a handsome prince,' Lu
replies.

We are agreed then, Lu and I. Theatre for me, a palace
for her.

Our coach driver talks with a funny accent that Mrs
Stanley says is American. He has long sideburns and wears
dark glasses. Mrs Stanley blushes red when she talks to him.
She says he looks like Elvis.

They obviously have funny-looking elves in America.

'Here y'all are kids. Y'all have a good time now, yessiree.'

We enter a large hall, festooned with bunches of red and
green balloons and red crepe-paper streamers. Long trestle
tables are laid out with an impressive festive tea.

But the bad side of the party is that we have to share it
with the children from the spastics' home. If we are in any
doubt about our position it is clarified by a banner hanging
halfway across the room:

Welcome to the Spastics and Homeless Children
Merry Christmas

The highlight of the afternoon is the appearance of Father Christmas.

'Kathy Abbott.'

Not for the first time, I'm grateful that God gave me a surname beginning with A.

Father Christmas calls my sisters' names. We all get the same thing: a necklace-making kit with plastic beads of every colour. Tigs, of course, bargains for something more useful and gets a cricket bat.

Fleetingly, it occurs to me that perhaps they got a job lot of presents from the back-of-a-lorry shop. This thought is followed uncomfortably by a brief memory of my father. What is he doing this Christmas? Where is he? The thought makes me feel bad. I thrust it away. I don't want to think about him.

I turn my attention to the spastic girl next to me. The seating arrangements are one able-bodied child, one spastic child, one able-bodied child and so forth. The able-bodied children are supposed to help the spastic children.

The girl next to me gets a necklace kit as well. I look at her closely. She's about the same age as me. Her hair is thick and shiny, like it's just been washed, but it's been cut in an ugly wedge. I feel sorry for her. She tries to eat her beads so I try to explain their function to her.

Her helper comes over and takes the beads away. 'For God's sake, whose idea was it to give them beads? They'll choke to death.'

The girl begins to howl. Louder and louder, louder and louder. Desperately, I put one of the fairy cakes in her hand.

The girl takes the fairy cake and starts mashing it about. She grins at me, making some other groany noises like she's trying to talk. I smile back but really, I am desperately hoping she won't actually touch me with her mashy-dribbly hand.

When it's time to leave, the spastic kids clump out on their sticks or in their wheelchairs, with their helpers pushing and wiping and getting cross.

We, the able-bodied, watch and although wards of the state, count our blessings.

The high point of our Christmas is my mother's visit. She arrives looking incredibly groovy, wearing a whiter than white woolly sweater, with a red chiffon scarf and red slacks. Her hair is high, backcombed and crispy to the touch.

'Why is your hair crispy?'

'That's the hairspray. It keeps it in place.'

Behind my mother's hair is my nanny's grey bobbing head. I am overjoyed.

'Nanny!'

'Hullo dearies. Hullo Kathy dear.'

I bury my face first into Mummy's lap and then into my beloved nanny's. My mother smells of perfume, whereas Nanny smells of fresh baking and soap.

Nanny and Mummy, like the three kings, have come laden with gifts. Nanny unloads at least fifty mince pies and Christmas stockings full to the brim with chocolate and sweets. We tear everything open in a frenzy and eat and eat.

I scoff more than my fair share of mince pies, which my sisters don't like, and pocket several for Louis.

'Let's have a Christmas photo, girls,' says my mother.

So we line up.

'Now one with you and Nanny … say leek.'

With all this Christmas cheer about, I decide it's a good time to bring up my adopt-a-Louis plan. My mother laughs uproariously at the suggestion. 'Good heavens, what an idea! As if four children aren't enough.'

'Does that mean no?' I ask.

'Darling,' says my mother, 'you're my children. I can't worry about anybody else's, can I?'

'I hate you!' I say, and skulk in the corner of the hut.

'Don't be like that Kathy,' says Nanny. 'It's Christmas.'

But I won't be consoled. After all, what will Louis do if he has to stay here forever?

'He won't always be a child, Kathy, he'll grow up and he can leave then.'

My mother's summing-up of Louis' future nearly kills me. He has nothing, and when he eventually leaves here he will go to nothing.

I turn my face to the wall.

At the visit's end, my mother bends down and looks in my face. 'Won't you say goodbye, Kathy? Give me a cuddle?'

'No!' I say and turn away. 'Not if we can't look after Louis.'

'Happy Christmas, Kathy,' Nanny pats my shoulder. I pull away, sulking. Nanny and Mummy turn to hug my sisters and then they all go outside.

After a few seconds, my resolve cracks and I run outside to say goodbye too.

But they haven't waited. I'm in time to see the taxi pull

away. I catch a glimpse of the back of my nanny's grey head, and my mother's crispy hairdo almost touching the inside roof of the car. The vehicle exhaust fumes hang in the air like fog. All that's left are the tyre tracks in the earth and the angry cawing of crows from the field.

My sisters and I trail back to the house.

Christmas morning dawns and to my utmost astonishment on each child's bed is a pillowcase chock-full of presents. I've never seen so many presents in all my life. If the currency of a child's life is sweets and presents, then we, the poor and unwanted, have hit the mother lode. There is everything: Lego, Etch A Sketches in red plastic, Tiny Tears dollies, colouring-in pens, colouring-in books, comic annuals, compendiums of games, red and white crepe Christmas stockings stuffed with confectionery – Milky Way bars, Caramac chocolate, Hula Hoops and Bounty bars. There must be an explanation for all this unbelievable good fortune.

'It's to make up for not having parents,' explains Louis.

It occurs to me that strictly speaking I do have parents. I explain this to Louis. 'Does that mean I'll have to give my presents back?' I ask.

Louis considers this, leaning his brown head to one side. 'I don't think so, because if Father Christmas – like you know, in person – came all the way from the North Pole to put a pillowcase on your bed, then he must know what he's doing, mustn't he?'

Once the frenzy of paper-ripping and opening is over, we get on with the real business of swapping presents.

'I'll swap you my Chinese chequers for your Tiny Tears.'
No deal. No one likes Chinese chequers.

Poor Tigs has her work cut out because she's got a pillow-case full of detestable 'girl' presents. She accosts the boys trying vainly to swap her Tiny Tears for a Meccano set.

Bud finally relinquishes her Spiky doll for a new Barbie and relegates Spiky to the bin. Even I feel a bit sorry for Spiky, what with her head in the rubbish and her stiff plastic legs sticking up.

I later discover that my father came on that Christmas Day and parked down the lane. He sat in his van smoking cigarettes and hoping for a glimpse of his children. As the winter sun broke through, the Pilgrim House children poured outside to work off the sugar overload. Did he see us? I don't know the answer, I only know that he was there. The superintendent spotted the van and called the police.

When I learn this I ask her, 'Did my daddy want to kidnap us?'

She shook her head. 'I don't know. Perhaps he just wanted to give you Christmas presents. We'll never know, but we can't take the chance can we?'

The glories of Christmas fade. Pilgrim House returns to its routine. January, February, the months pass.

In March Tigs and I turn nine years old. We each receive a birthday card from our father. Inside my card my father wrote only, 'Love Daddy.'

Tigs and I look at each other. We don't mention the cards. We put them aside.

Later, when I am alone, I take the card out. I look at his writing, 'Love Daddy.' Inside me there is a longing, a wanting. I want my father to love me. I want it all to be all right. I want 'home' with my mother and father, even though I know that it has ceased to exist.

Deliverance

Imagine if you will a glossy, gleaming, Rolls-Royce. Imagine a chauffeur, dressed in a dark overcoat and cap, and a beautiful woman buttoning a mink coat and wrapping a white scarf around her neck. Imagine this, and you are seeing my mother arriving at Pilgrim House.

There is no warning. We have spent a rainy morning inside. The playroom has the stuffy fug about it that rooms do when full of repressed children. The superintendent opens the door and calls, 'The Abbott children!'

Once outside the playroom the superintendent looks us up and down. 'Your mother is here. You're going home.'

We gaze at her with our mouths open. Bud, Lu, Tigs and I exchange looks. Can she possibly mean what she's saying?

'Hurry up. Your mother's waiting.'

Our things have already been packed up and stand waiting in the hall, no doubt part of the 'secret visitor' policy. We are whirled outside in the blink of an eye.

There is my mother, smiling broadly. We hurl ourselves

at her, there is no force stronger. Four sets of eyes and mouths and arms and legs.

'Are we really going home?' asks Bud, her eyes shining.

'Yes.'

How can I describe the joy, the happiness, the fantasticness of it? Tigs, Lu and I hold hands and grin at each other. We jump up and down.

The chauffeur eyes us somewhat coolly as he opens the door to the car, allowing us in. Bud pulls up her socks and neatly slides along the padded leather seat. Tigs tucks her collected sports goods under her arm and slides along next to her. Lu flicks back her hair, as if to the manor born, and I get in last, taking the seat by the window.

It is only when we drive away that I realise I haven't said goodbye to Louis or anyone else. Do I see him or does my guilty conscience see him, his bobbly brown head peering from the window of Pilgrim House?

We speed along the highways of England in the Rolls-Royce. It is smooth, indulgent; it has electric windows, which we buzz up and down repeatedly.

We arrive at our new home. There must be some mistake. It is not a house, not even part of a house but a flatette around the back of someone else's house. It is new, immaculately furnished, but there is only one bedroom.

'Where will we all sleep, Mummy?' asks Lu, a bit taken aback. Lu had already prepared herself for a four-poster bed in our new mansion.

'Girls, there is someone I want you to meet. His name is Francis.'

Francis is tall. He has dark brown hair and dark brown eyes fringed with impossibly thick black lashes. He is, perhaps, about forty years of age, and dressed, like my father, in a good suit. His voice is remarkable, like thick chocolate, soothing and soft. A Dutch chocolate accent. As much as we are poor, Francis, like his accent, is patently rich.

'Hello children. I've heard very good things about you.' He produces a giant Toblerone bar with triangles the size of your hand. 'I picked it up in duty free for you. I believe you like chocolate.'

As we tuck in to the chocolate, Francis stands over me, watching. 'Kathy, isn't it?'

'Yes.'

'What's wrong with your feet?'

'What do you mean?'

'You walk on your toes.'

I blush. Even he noticed.

'Have you ever seen a doctor about it?'

Bud intervenes. 'She's always walked like that.'

Francis looks around at my mother and my sisters and then back to me. 'We'll see if we can fix that.' He leans down and pats me on the head.

I look up into his face. I wonder what he means exactly.

'Mummy, is he our new daddy?' Lu asks, with a vested interest in maintaining a Toblerone supply.

Francis laughs. 'Not exactly.'

I like Francis. I like his manner, he is gentle and quiet.

'No, he's not your new daddy, exactly … he's my friend.

I want you all to be very good. Okay?'

'Okay,' Lu, Bud, Tigs and I nod.

My mother's new love is Francis Van Seumeran, a Dutch millionaire and staunch Catholic. Well, staunch in all but one respect. Love may indeed know no boundaries but, technically, Francis is already a married man with nine children living a hop, skip and a jump away in Holland. Francis skips to London regularly, on more than just business.

Needless to say, the life of a man and his mistress is seriously compromised by the presence of four young children. A solution has to be found.

'We're going on holiday!' my mother says.

Mummy helps us pack. We have new everything, including four sets of school uniforms. These uniforms aren't like any I've seen, they are clearly expensive. We have camel raincoats, silver and blue blazers, silver and blue Juliet caps, white gloves, and brown real leather shoes. These are just the tip of the iceberg. We have new towels, new bedding, new sheets, new brushes, new play-clothes, new underwear, new stationery. New everything from toothbrushes to tinned shoe polish.

Who bankrolled all this bounty we did not know. It just was. Just as it was that we departed for a holiday to a place called Middleton-on-Sea.

'We should call it Puddleton-on-Sea,' jokes my mother, looking out at the relentless rain.

We stay in a self-contained holiday bungalow. There's a bedroom for us girls, and one for Mummy. It's very cream and brown and neat and tidy but there's not much to do with the weather being so bad.

We play 'bored' (board) games until we're sick of the sight of them. When the rain lets up briefly we head for the beach, but it's still too damp, so we play minigolf and eat seaside rock. At night we sit together eating fish and chips and sweets.

The final evening, my mother gets up and starts stacking up all our new clothing. She brings out some labels with our names printed on them.

'We have to have everything labelled for school tomorrow and that includes the towels and sheets.'

'Why do we have to label the sheets?' says Bud. 'It's not like we're sleeping at school, is it?'

Mummy looks a bit funny.

'Girls,' she says, 'I want you to know you're going to boarding school. It's a lovely place and you'll be happy there, and you get to come home in the holidays.'

My sisters and I look at each other.

'But Mummy,' says Tigs desperately, 'we want to stay with you.'

Mummy looks at Tigs, at Lu and Bud and me.

'I know you do, darlings, but it's not right yet. Once you get settled into your school you'll see it's all for the best.'

That night I lie in my bed thinking about what my mother has said.

And the next day we are delivered with new haircuts to boarding school.

*

My boarding-school life starts with a view through the car window. Think of a traditional English village with Tudor houses and narrow streets. Think of hedgerows of autumn leaves and blackberries.

'Our' car, with the faintly disapproving chauffeur, pulls up at a Tudor mansion. St Joseph's Dominican Convent. Its mullioned windows twinkle like a myriad diamonds in the autumn sunshine.

As we get out of the car, two ladies in long white dresses come out to greet us. 'Nuns', it seems, wear long dresses all the time, like uniforms. (Habits I am later to learn.) The older lady-in-white introduces herself. 'I'm Sister Lutgardis. This is Sister Delores.' Sister Delores is pretty with an inch of red hair showing under her veil. 'Welcome.'

My sisters and I exchange looks at this first public use of our new name.

My mother and the chauffeur collect our suitcases from the car.

'Now let me see,' Sister Lutgardis continues, 'this must be the eldest. Bud, isn't it? And the twins, and who is this young lady?' She bends down and looks straight into Lu's anxious hazel eyes. 'Ah. I can see you're worried. Don't be. It's all new but you'll see there's lots of other children to play with and lots to learn and lots of fun to be had.'

Sister Lutgardis chuckles. 'Come on in little chicks and we'll get you settled. Say goodbye to your mummy.'

Stricken, we turn to our mother.

She looks equally troubled.

'Mummy ...'

'Bud,' says my mother, 'I want you to look after your sisters for me.'

Bud nods but there are tears welling in her eyes.

'Mummy ...'

'Come on girls. I'll be down to see you every week. Every week.' My mother unclings our hands from her body. Sister Lutgardis takes Lu and Tigs by the hand and starts walking inside.

'Go on Bud, Kathy. Go on now.'

Bud and I stand in the doorway, hesitating. My mother pulls herself up.

'Don't forget I love you. Be good.'

My mother turns and walks back to the waiting chauffeur. With nothing else to do Bud and I follow Sister Lutgardis.

Inside the entrance hall of carved stone is a long gallery with a balcony. 'That is where the minstrels used to play,' Sister Lutgardis tells us. I'm not sure what she means; the only minstrels I know of are Galaxy chocolate ones with a crispy coating, and I couldn't imagine them getting up there to play.

The house is huge. We follow Sister Lutgardis up a curved flight of wooden stairs. From a lofty position above an archway the cold glass eyes of a stuffed stag head, complete with antlers, follow our progress. We arrive in a long sunlit room at the top of the stairs.

'This is your bedroom, girls.'

Not at all like the Pilgrim House dormitory, which was overcrowded, this room has only six beds in it. It is huge, with polished floors and window seats. The adjoining bathroom is massive and has white tiles and a bathtub big enough to swim in. I look out the window on to manicured green lawns and neatly trimmed hedges.

From a lifetime of poverty, of living in dark, poky rooms, it suddenly dawns on me that this is how the rich and privileged live, in high-ceilinged rooms with gracious views. More astonishing is the fact that I, Kathy Abbott, am here at all. My sisters and I look at each other in disbelief.

'We've kept you in together for the first term. We only have a few boarders here and we'd like you to think of us as a big family. I'll leave you to unpack your things and get settled and then I'll take you on a quick tour after tea. I'm sure you have lots of questions to ask.'

For a stunned moment my sisters and I sit in this palatial room and watch arcs of light dance across the polished floors. It truly seems as if we have landed on another planet.

Sometime later a boy with a mop of dark brown hair arrives. His socks are rolled down and he has quite a few promising-looking scabs on his knees. These do not go unnoticed by Tigs, who is always impressed by such trophies.

'I'm Dominic from Ireland. Sister Delores sent me to get you because we're running late for tea.'

We look at Dominic.

'Aw hurry up. You'll miss tea an' 'tis always good on the first night back.'

We follow Dominic down the wooden stairway and he fills us in on the essentials. 'Now be sure to serve yourself straightaway because if you wait, all that's left will be the greens, and sure you shouldn't have to be eating those till you're grown and married ... After grace is finished, of course.'

'What's grace?' inquires Bud.

Dominic looks at us somewhat alarmed. 'Don't you know what grace is?'

We shake our heads.

'Why the whole world knows it's when you sit down to a meal and thank the Lord for all his gifts.'

'Gifts?' Lu's eyes light up. 'You mean we'll get presents?'

'No, no.' Dominic eyes us, slightly exasperated. 'Sure, you know, 'tis a sin not to say grace.'

'What's a sin?' I ask, trying to remember where I'd read about such things.

Dominic gasps. 'Have you no religion?'

We shake our heads; apparently not.

Dominic rubs his hands, thrilled; he breathes one word, 'Heathens!'

By the end of the week I have pretty much got an idea of this sin business. I also have a grasp of boarding-school routine and the fact that the nuns are all pretty keen on God. In fact they're all married to Him.

And it's very nice to have a holy nun tuck you into bed and say a goodnight prayer with you. It makes you feel safe.

As I lay me down to sleep
I pray the Lord my soul to keep.

On Saturday mornings we are allowed to walk down to the village and spend our weekly pocket money at the sweetshop.

'Not sweets,' Dominic says, 'coconuts are the thing.' He waves his hands. 'Have you never had a piece of tender coconut on your tongue? 'Tis better than chocolate, chewier than toffee, and there's milk in the middle for your thirst, and it lasts longer. Why, a coconut is everything rolled into one.'

Persuaded by the lilting tones of my new Irish friend, I pool my money with his and we purchase from the grocers a coconut the size of a shrunken head. The outside is brown and hairy.

'It doesn't look very good,' I say to Dominic.

'Ah, wait till we open it.'

We get back to school with the mysterious fruit. It soon becomes obvious that Dominic has overlooked the fact that we have nothing to open the coconut with.

He scratches his head. 'I know. We'll smash it against the stones.'

We spend the next hour taking it in turns trying to smash our coconut. Finally, with a crack, the shell opens and the milk soaks into the ground.

'Oh no!'

We try to retrieve the milk but it's too late. Only slightly daunted, Dominic picks up the broken pieces of coconut.

I pick up a piece. 'It smells funny.' I gnaw at my piece and spit it out in disgust.

Our coconut has an unpromising mouldy-brown

interior and tastes foul. Dominic spits his out. We are bitterly disappointed.

'Bloody rotten thing,' he yells, kicking what's left of the coconut into the bushes.

'I'm hungry,' I say.

'Come on, let's go and find Mr Seeteck.' Dominic sets off at a pace somewhere between running and really running.

'Who is Mr Seeteck?' I ask, puffing and trying to keep up.

'You'll see.'

Dominic leads me behind the school to a maze of sheds filled with shelves of apples. Apples of every size and colour. Fresh apples, mouldering apples, dried apples. Apples everywhere.

'There he is. Hi Mr Seeteck!' Dominic waves.

Mr Seeteck wears a flat cap and his skin is the same tone as the russet-coloured apples. 'What ho. If it isn't young Dom. Have a good holiday?'

'Not really,' says Dominic, then changes the subject. 'This is Kathy. She's new and she's a heathen.'

'Is she now?' Mr Seeteck eyes me. 'Would you like an apple?'

Mr Seeteck hands us a couple of apples with his big brown hands.

'Mr Seeteck. Could we have a ride? See ...'

Dominic launches into a long and emotional tale about our rotten coconut.

Mr Seeteck listens with an expression of concern, then says, 'All right then, come on.'

We follow Mr Seeteck to his tractor. He lets us sit in the tray on the back.

'Hold on tight.'

Mr Seeteck lifts the tray up and down. We scream with delight. After a few minutes he turns off the engine.

'There you are then. I've got to get back to work before it gets dark.'

'Thank you, Mr Seeteck,' I say breathlessly.

'I'm glad you're settling in. See you later.'

We scamper off.

'See,' says Dominic. 'You never need to be hungry, Kathy.'

I nod. Dominic and I run back up to the school. I am looking forward to telling Tigs and Lu. I don't know about Bud, she would say the tractor ride was dangerous and box my ears.

Monday morning brings something called a catechism lesson. According to Dominic, this is about religion. Tigs sits looking a little bit concerned in a desk near the back. Because I'm brave, or actually partly blind, I sit in a desk near the front. David, who has crutches, sits next to me. I'm not sure what's wrong with David exactly. He's quite sweet but it is impossible to talk to him after recess, because he gets the worst milk breath in Christendom.

Our class is led by Father Cassidy who lives in the monastery down the road. Father Cassidy has a curious round face with a turned-up nose, a little bit like a snout. You can't help but think that if he was caught in the rain he'd probably drown.

'Good morning, boys and girls.'

'Good morning, Father Cassidy.'

'Now, I think the Sisters have asked me to review our work last term on the lives of the saints ... Who can tell me about Saint Patrick?'

A smattering of hands go up. Not Tigs, of course, who only puts her hand up to be selected in a team.

One girl, with spectacles and a superior air, launches into a summary: 'He's the patron saint of Ireland and he got rid of all the snakes in Ireland and he has a holy place in heaven on the right with Our Lord.'

'Um. Yes. Well you seem to have a grasp on the saints. So would you like a little story ... I've heard a very good one ...'

'Yes!'

'Gather round then.'

Father Cassidy leans in and begins his yarn. 'It was a cold and stormy night. As usual, the hobgoblins were up stealing socks and putting slugs in the lettuces, but across in the graveyard, where the dead sleep and mist swirls even in the middle of the day ...'

As Father Cassidy tells his scary tale, we squirm and scream. We scream so loud that Sister Lutgardis puts her head around the door and eyes our flushed faces, all huddled around Father Cassidy's knees.

'Is everything all right, Father?'

'Oh indeed, Sister Lutgardis. I think they are just moved by the Holy Spirit.'

Father Cassidy winks. 'I believe it's morning break,' he says.

Outside, Father Cassidy strolls with us into the sunshine. He joins in with us in pretending to be horses, jumping over the hedge. It's quite a sight to see Father Cassidy neighing and jumping over the hedge in his long copper robes.

'I'm a not a piebald but a friar-bald,' he snorts. 'Get it? A bit short on mane.' He pats his shiny bald head.

Sister Delores comes flitting across the lawn to offer Father Cassidy morning tea. Like all the sisters, she treats him exceedingly reverently. It might be because he's God's servant, but I think it's because he's a man. I glimpse him in the nuns' parlour, encircled by sisters fluttering around him like white butterflies.

On Sunday my mother arrives for our weekend visit. There she is waiting in the visitors' parlour. She is dressed in a tight jumper and her black hair is up, backcombed and crispy.

She has also magically acquired a larger pair of bosoms. They are perfectly symmetrical rounds, exactly like coconut-halves.

'They're new,' says Bud.

'What?' I ask. 'Did they just pop up?'

'With a bit of help from the doctor, if you must know.'

'But why?' asks Lu.

'To make them ... better.'

We try to digest this information.

Bud reaches in to touch my mother's new bosoms. 'But they're hard!' she says.

My mother wrestles out of our grasp. 'For goodness' sake,

can we change the subject? I've come all this way to see you and I don't want to talk about my … my bosoms, okay?'

My mother sits down again, looks at us. 'So how's school, how are you settling in?'

'It's all right,' says Bud, 'but can we come home?'

'Soon. In the school holidays.' My mother steers the conversation back to school.

'I see you're learning to say your aitches.'

'Yeah. And it's th-under not funder. It's th-ink not fink,' offers Tigs. Practically a speech for her.

'Great. You should learn to speak properly. Now the sisters say there's a good teashop in the village. Shall we go and get something to eat?'

We walk down to the village; it's a cold day, with a weak sun barely warming the air. We enter the teashop, which has a tinkling bell on the door. There are four or five dark wooden tables laid with white napkins and plates. A lady emerges from the gloom at the back and smiles at us.

'Five of you?' She pulls two tables together to make six places and gives us hand-written menus.

'Are you from the convent?' the lady asks. Oh, so observant. We are in school uniform.

'Yes,' says my mother. 'What would you like to eat, girls?'

We settle for Welsh rarebit and cakes from the trolley.

We eat until we feel sick. My mother sips her tea and pushes a cake around her plate.

'I'm on a diet,' she says. 'I can't eat this.'

'What's a diet?' I ask.

'Oh, it's when you want to lose weight and so you don't eat fattening foods like cream cake.'

'What for? You're not fat,' I say.

'Kathy. You don't stay slim if you eat too much.'

'Yes,' says Bud, 'I hope you're taking notes, Kathy.'

'Shut up.'

Bud aims a punch at my ear but misses, knocking a teacup to the floor.

'Girls! Stop it!'

Bud and I glower at each other across the table. Tigs squirrels away half the cheesecake for later. She still saves things in her pockets.

'Come on,' my mother says, 'let's go for a walk.'

She pays the bill and we lead her along the river and back down past the village shop. At the shop she buys us little gifts. I get a cardboard case with a lock, Lu chooses a book of transfers, Bud some bracelets and Tigs a yoyo.

'Something to remember me by in the week.'

We walk back up to the convent, knowing that the visit is over. My mother looks at her watch, her driver pulls up on time. Four o'clock.

We stand in the drive as the evening darkens and the lights of the convent brighten. There is a melancholy smell of leaves and garden bonfires. My mother waves from the car window.

'Be good girls. I love you.'

We drag our feet up the steps and into the school.

*

The next day, we take our resentment out on the day students. The ones who get to go home to their mums and dads after school.

'Day-dog at three o'clock eating packed lunch.'

With a roar, several boarders rush the hapless day pupil. We are all armed with bunches of stinging nettles.

'Ow! Ow! Stop it!' The day pupil hops about trying to dodge us. 'What did I do? I wasn't doing anything ...'

The day pupil runs off howling, looking for a teacher. 'I'm going to tell ...'

'C'mon chaps, better scat ...'

We run as far and fast as we are able.

Dominic and I find ourselves at the perimeter of the local farm. The farm is out of bounds.

With childish awe, we watch the men, labourers, in their work overalls. They seem to inhabit a strange masculine world. A world of rolled-up sleeves, of sweat, cigarette smoke, labour and muscle. The cigarette smoke wafts up past us, and suddenly I am reminded of my father.

'Do you miss your dad?' I ask Dominic. Dominic's parents are dead.

Dominic looks at me. 'You know, I can't remember his face or my mum's ... only a lonely kind of feeling.'

We are silent for a bit.

'Do you miss yours?'

'I dunno,' I say. 'My dad didn't like me very much.'

Dominic looks at me. 'Why's that?'

'Don't know. I can't remember his face any more either.'

'We should get back to school.' I turn away from the men and Dominic follows.

Back at school, I go to my 'sanctuary' to be alone. This is an attic room stuffed full of costumes from all the school plays from all the years and all the thrills of St Joseph school productions. There are Little Bo-Peep dresses and queenly robes, there are scarves and swords and hats with flowers. Props from forgotten dramas: tea sets, stuffed animals, cardboard crowns, candlesticks, guns, angel wings and feather boas.

I observe myself in the mirror. Here I am, Kathy Abbott. What do I see? Short brown hair, a fringe, green eyes, pale skin. What is it about me that is so unlovely and unlovable? I feel tears prick my eyes and turn away from the mirror. I pick up a hat; for a little while I can pretend to be someone else.

I pretend to be someone else very successfully in the school play of St George and the Dragon. I play the Fool and wear a harlequin costume. The local newspaper takes a photograph. I stand at the front of the stage wielding a dagger in a suitably dramatic pose. Fame at last!

'I look more beautiful,' Lu says.

She's right, she does. She looks like a princess.

Tigs hides her stage fright under a white beard and black cloak. She makes a most unconvincing old doctor, although her quaking limbs are genuine.

Perhaps it's the sight of us on stage that prompts the matter of our mortal souls to arise (so to speak). Sister Lutgardis accosts me in the corridor.

'Kathy. I think it's time you all joined God's family.'

'Yes, Sister.' (What with the shortfall in my own, I don't mind having a heavenly father.)

'Your mother says she can arrange extra catechism lessons in the holidays and that you can be baptised at your local church.'

'Yes, Sister.'

'Good. That's settled. We can't have you and your sisters wandering around in mortal danger any longer. Anything could happen.'

'Yes, Sister.'

The site of our spiritual debut is the Sacred Heart Church, Wimbledon, near my mother's new flat (in a block of four called Marlowe House). This flat is large enough for us to stay during school holidays.

The Sacred Heart Church, if it still exists, is a draughty Gothic building the size of a cinema, but not as entertaining. Sister Margaret has been given the job of converting a group of child heathens on Wednesday afternoons. Sister Margaret searches our souls with her dark eyes.

'Faith. It is the cornerstone of belief. Without it you cannot be a Catholic. Do you have faith, Kathy Abbott?'

'I … I think I'm starting to,' I reply, looking desperately across at a good-looking boy called Llewellyn.

This Llewellyn appears incredibly sophisticated. He wears a white silk scarf which contrasts startlingly with his dark skin and matches his dazzling white teeth. Lu, Tigs and I watch him in awe.

It's lucky Bud is not here as she'd probably eat him for

breakfast. (Bud has decided to eschew religion in favour of boys.)

'Girls and boys, I'd like to introduce you to Father Strahan, who is going to be baptising you,' says Sister Margaret.

Father Strahan is a mid-sized man wearing a hat. This is a surprise as it's not often you see a priest in a hat. He tips it politely at us and says hello.

'Now would be a good opportunity to ask Father any questions you might have about the ceremony itself.'

My sisters and I aren't confident enough to put up our hands, but Llewellyn at the back raises his in a lordly fashion.

'I say Father, will the baptismal water be heated?'

Father Strahan eyes Llewellyn. Sister Margaret looks embarrassed.

'I'll think you'll find the water will be room temperature, young man.'

There's an embarrassed silence as no further questions are forthcoming. With a disappointed air Father Strahan turns on his heel and departs.

On Saturday, Lu, Tigs and I arrive for our spiritual awakening. In view of the shortage of godparents, the Ferraris, a local Italian couple, have offered to stand in.

My mother, my sisters and I group in a faintly embarrassed clump outside the church. There is no sign of Llewellyn, who has perhaps found he has an aversion to conversion, or room-temperature water.

We are to be baptised and, thus free of sin, receive our first Holy Communion at the mass straight afterwards. This production-line approach offends Lu's sense of how things should be done.

'It's all very hit-and-miss,' she exclaims, 'look, we haven't even got special dresses.'

It's true, we do look a bit stupid in veils and normal clothes.

As we wait, we see Father Strahan in his car motoring towards us. His car goes no faster than a trot, he should get a 'slow' ticket rather than a speeding ticket.

This lack of speed is reflected in the ceremony itself. Father Strahan takes his time. Our mortal souls teeter on the brink, until finally, 'I baptise ... you ... in ... the ... name ... of ... the ... er ... Father ... the ... er Son ... and ... the ... Holy ... Ghost.'

My mother flaps uncomfortably like a duck out of water. Doubting Bud takes on the role of the proud mother, I look expectant, Tigs fidgets in her dress, Lu wears an expression which seems to say, 'I hope no one sees me, least of all God.'

Immediately after my induction into the Catholic faith, it's time to attend my first confession. The very next day I am at the church door. In fact, I spend most of the rest of the holidays in church or, more accurately, the confessional. I have become a confessional professional.

'Bless me, Father, for I have sinned. It has been three hours since my last confession ...'

'Do you not think, child, that you might not need to confess again today? It's a lovely day, you might want to go swimming ...'

'Oh no, Father. I have to confess. There isn't a limit, is there?'

'Er ... no.'

I can't see the priest behind the screen, but I can hear him turning pages. If I didn't know better I'd swear he was reading a novel.

Returning to my mother's flat from my umpteenth confession, I find Francis and my mother sitting in the dining room. He is dressed immaculately. I feel a little bit awkward. Francis regards me.

'You'll see your faith will always be something you can rely on.' Francis pulls his rosary out of his pocket, and smiles.

After Francis has gone my mother gives me a grey felt box. On the satin inside is a gold cross studded with turquoise. It is delicate and beautiful.

'It's from Francis and me. I helped pick it,' my mother says.

'It's lovely. Thank you.'

I put the cross around my neck. It is like a glow in my heart. Maybe I'm not so bad after all?

Back at school, preparations begin almost immediately for the end-of-term open day and fundraiser.

'We thought it would be a fine idea for the boarders to create their own choral speaking group. There'll be practice on Tuesdays after study,' Sister Lutgardis informs us as she pins up a list in the common room.

As we have little in the way of a social life we cluster around the notice.

'What's choral speaking?' whispers Tigs, who has only just found the confidence to speak at all and is still intimidated by the idea of making a noise in public. She examines an unsavoury-looking clump from her pocket and offers it to me.

'Er, no thanks.'

'Dominic? What's choral speaking then?'

''Tis not talking and 'tis not singing, 'tis like a compromise between the two.'

I say, 'What's the point of that then?'

Dominic accepts Tigs' offer of the clump and starts to chew. 'Oh well, there's no point to it. Old people seem to like it. What is this then, Tigs, cheese?'

Tigs looks a bit uncertain.

'I hope there's a part for me,' Lu says.

'And I should be allowed to organise it,' says Bud. 'I'll talk to Sister Lutgardis.'

Bud marches off with her small posse of deputies. She, single-minded, and they, with no minds at all, have found each other.

'You get biscuits and hot chocolate after practice, if my memory serves,' Dominic says.

Hastily I pencil my name on to the list.

'Give it your all, boarders, remember to emphasise the p's!' Sister Lutgardis exhorts us as we stand before the bishop himself, along with parents, friends and sundry vassals of the Holy Roman Church.

We are the opening act of open day.

My mother has arrived in a gypsy-ish summer dress and lilac sandals. She's the standout mother of the day. Even the bishop comes up to say hello and look down the front of her dress.

Those bosoms have a magnetic effect.

Spare a penny, spare a penny, spare a penny,
   PLEEEEESE.
From your many, many PENCE, spare me one or two
   or threeeeeeeeeeeeee.
See my clothes are all in rags and I'd like a cup of tea-
   eeeeeee.

Our choral presentation is followed by the kindergarten children dressed up as blackbirds and sitting in a cardboard pie.

They are supposed to sing a stirring rendition of 'Sing a Song of Sixpence' but get collective stage fright. The little blackbirds don't sing a note and just sit in their pie blinking, beaks gaping, at the audience. One child starts to sob and in a panic, lest there be some sort of chain reaction, their teacher starts to sing 'Twinkle, Twinkle Little Star'. This sets off a confused medley of nursery classics – 'London Bridge Is Falling Down', 'Row, Row, Row Your Boat', 'Frere Jacques' and 'Incy Wincy Spider'. The scheduled 'Sing a Song of Sixpence' is overlooked in the panic.

This never-to-be-repeated performance is followed by a gymnastics display. Then Dominic gives a sublime recital of 'Danny Boy' for Holy Ireland, but there's trouble with the PA and no one can hear him.

All the while the sisters creep about, prompting desperately, as if no one can see them in their white habits in the sunshine.

The show must go on (and on). Just as it seems that the parents and students can bear no more, Sister Lutgardis announces the prize-giving.

'The sports cup this year has been awarded to …'

Tigs gives a start behind me as her name is called.

'Go on,' I nudge her. 'Go on.'

For the first time in her life Tigs walks out in front of people. She keeps her eyes on the grass and barely lifts them to collect the cup, but her face is brimful with pride. It's about time she got a bit of praise.

'The drama cup is awarded to Kathy Abbott.'

By jingo, I jump up and scoot over to the prize table before anyone can change their mind.

'Well done, Kathy, well done.'

I look across at my sisters who are grinning like loonies and my mother, who is becomingly flushed with pride. I look up at the peerless blue sky, a perfect moment in a perfect summer's day. Every dog has his day. This is mine.

'Colditz'

We return home with the disapproving chauffeur for the school holidays.

It transpires that we have moved again. Our new address is a renovated flat above a beauty salon. It is a three-storey building with the flat occupying two floors – the living area on the first floor and three bedrooms above that.

And it's not just any beauty salon, but our mother's. It has the words 'Marie's Beauty Salon' painted in large white letters at the front.

This is not a wise move if you don't want people (like my father) to know where you are.

'I'm going to be a beauty therapist,' my mother tells us proudly, brandishing several textbooks. 'I've been doing a course.'

To prove it, after dinner she dyes our eyelashes. I look in the mirror, astonished at what a bit of tint can do. Bud, Lu, Tigs and I bat our eyelashes at each other.

The flat above the salon is newly decorated. There's a plush green velvet sofa with tassels, a marble dining table with a Tiffany lamp overhead. A huge golden-framed mirror hangs above the mantelpiece.

Lu and Bud share one bedroom, Tigs and I the other. Everything is new; new beds, new quilts, new towels. It is not spoken about but understood that Francis is once again our benefactor.

'We've arranged for you to go on girl guide camp,' our mother says. 'It's only for a few weeks, while I work to pass my exams.'

So Lu, Tigs and I are hastily enrolled in the local girl guides. (It's amazing what a donation can do to expedite matters.) And we are packed off on the train for girl guide camp. Bud is allowed to stay home.

The camp is run by a ruddy-faced woman with stouter legs than mine. (Walking on your toes gives you calves any Tudor would be proud of.)

'Tally ho, gels, let's get the tents up.' We are somewhere in the country in the middle of a big green field. 'Kathy, you're in "Badger".'

My sisters are put in different groups and tents. I feel a bit upset about being separated; is it an omen?

Unfortunately, the charm of a girl guide camp is lost on me.

'Ging-gang-gooley-gooley-gooley-gooley-wash-gang, ging-gang-gooo, ging-gang-goooo ...'

There's something wrong with me because I can't get worked up about: 1) Sitting around in the cold singing stupid songs, 2) Useless activities like knitting with grass or climbing rope bridges.

The other girls, including my sisters, are taken up in a frenzy of earning points and badges. Tigs is fearless over the rope bridge, Lu has discovered a bent for homemaking and our tent is shipshape. I just want to go home and read.

'Dumpy wart legs, wet lettuce, fatty grimble.' Out of the blue even my sisters start taunting me with this new nickname.

We go on long treks. I start ahead of the others but soon trail behind, hoping they will leave me alone. I can't hide my despair when even Lu and Tigs join in.

'Dumpy wart legs, wet lettuce, fatty grimble.'

I am lonely without my sisters.

St Joseph's is no more; my junior school days are behind me. This is a tragedy. I loved St Joseph's as if it was my actual home. Was I never to see Dominic again? Sister Lutgardis? Sister Delores? Father Cassidy? The lovely sisters in white?

Our new destination is another boarding school.

Bud is attending day-school near my mother's flat – she and my mother have become great buddies. I am jealous, I'd like to stay home too but it is not possible.

'I can't work and have you all home, can I? Bud is a bit older and can do things for herself.'

Worse news is to come. Lu is to finish out a year at St Joseph's. We are all being separated.

'But Mummy, you can't leave Lu all by herself,' I say. 'I don't want her to be miles away, sleeping under a different roof.'

'Don't be silly Kathy. That's how it is now you're growing up.'

I'm amazed. I'm devastated. How can this be? I look at my sisters, Bud looks at me.

'It's all right, Kathy. It will be all right.'

'Yes,' adds my mother, 'and don't forget, you'll see each other in the holidays.'

The night before we are due to go to school, I sit with Lu on her bed. She's finishing packing, a new chequered set of towels, new shoes, Saturday 'home' clothes ... We are both miserable.

'I've got the phone number. You call me and I will call you.'

Lu nods. We both know that as kids, getting to use the telephone at school will be a rare occurrence. Tigs hovers by the door.

'I want you to have my pick-up sticks,' Tigs says as she gives Lu the game.

'It's all wrong,' says Lu. 'This isn't how families should be.' Bitter, desperate tears well up in her eyes. 'It's not fair!'.

'I love you,' I say and the three of us sit on the bed, holding each other.

Early the next morning, the chauffeur-driven car appears on cue to take Tigs and me to our new destination.

My mother tries to cheer us up. 'Come on, don't look so depressed. Just think how grown-up you are now!'

Tigs and I, our twelve-year-old selves, get into the car. We don't feel grown-up at all. I look through the window: my mother blows kisses and Bud waves, her lips pressed together with her pinched concerned look. Lu gazes at me silently, her eyes filled with despair. It's more than I can bear. Can't my mother see? Can't she see what's happening before her own eyes? An ache lodges in my heart. It finds a permanent emptiness, the place where Bud and Lu should be.

The Convent of the Blessed Sacrament, otherwise known as The Towers, is situated in the village of Upper Beeding. There is a curved drive and two stubby-looking towers. It looks like Colditz. The drive is full of girls in burgundy uniforms being deposited by parents.

Our chauffeur collects our cases from the car boot and gives them to us. He goes to get into the car but, as though he's had an afterthought, turns back, hesitating.

'Er … good luck, then.' It's the first time he has addressed us directly.

'Thanks.'

Tigs and I pick up our suitcases and walk up the steps and through the front door of our new school. The entrance hall is large with a curved staircase to the left.

A nun with a thick monobrow accosts us. (My mother with her new beauty therapy skills could probably pluck the brow into submission.) 'New boarders? Please go through to the gym and wait there.'

The gym is huge and inhospitable. There is a stage at one end and windows that look out at the darkening sky. Tigs and I stand together by the wall, feeling horrible. Everywhere there are strangers milling about. No one seems to notice us. There is no warm welcome and the nuns wear grey.

A bell sounds and, as if by magic, the crowd disperses. Someone yells 'refectory!'

By the time we find the refectory, tea is well under way. There are groups of girls sitting around octagonal-shaped tables. That's when I notice there are no boys. No Dominics to make you smile.

'Where have you been? You two can sit here.'

A frazzled sister points us to a table. There is not much tea left, only bread and jam. Memories of Pilgrim House wash over me. I look at Tigs miserably. She's thinking the same thing. All we want to do is go home.

After tea we are herded up to the dormitory to unpack and prepare for bed. The dormitory is a big room divided into thirty cubicles. Each girl has her own cubicle which is partitioned off with a curtain. The cubicles are identical – each containing a bed, a shelf, a chair, a tiny sink and a small cupboard.

Tigs' cubicle is a few curtains down from mine. She's put up a picture of the tennis champion Jimmy Connors. She has switched her allegiance from her football to male sportsmen.

I sit on my bed waiting patiently for a sister to come and tuck me in, like at St Joseph's. The light goes out suddenly. 'Goodnight girls,' someone calls and I realise with a jolt that that's all we're going to get.

'Goodnight Tigs,' I call out. She calls back, 'Goodnight Kaff.' I hunker down under the covers of my bed and feel extremely sorry for myself.

The Towers is an industry. It starts at seven in the morning when the dormitory mistress pulls the cubicle curtains back with a determined swipe. You can hear her moving down one side of the dormitory and back up the other, curtains thrown open, one after the other.

It's time to get up, brush our teeth, wash our faces and put on our uniforms, which we are meant to have laid out neatly on the chair, by the bottom of our beds. Mine, however, has inexplicably got crinkled up in my bedclothes.

Beds have to be made with proper 'hospital corners' and cubicles must be tidy. Once all this has been accomplished we can go down to breakfast.

Breakfast. In my mind's eye I had imagined chunky wedges of toast, eggs and bacon and a generous selection of cereals in miniature boxes like you get in hotels. Wrong.

The first thing that assails me as I enter the refectory is the overwhelming smell of a hundred boiled eggs. This unforgettable odour is offered up with sliced bread and dishes of fish fingers swimming in grease. As a veteran of the institutional life, I make sure I get a slice of bread by pressing my thumbs very hard into a top slice (possession being nine-tenths of the law). Accompanying this repast is an unlimited supply of tea and marmalade, which, if you mix in six or seven sugars, is reasonable. I am referring to the marmalade. The tea is beyond rescue.

In the light of day, I take in the people around me. The Towers is home to every kind of girl in the world. Pretty ones, plain ones, strange ones, older ones, younger ones, fat ones, thin ones. Girls all in the same fish-finger boat and not a Captain Birdseye fish-finger boat either, but some inferior brand.

After breakfast we go along to the chapel for prayers. I am hopeful of a cosy interview in the confessional but I am shocked to discover that boarders can only attend confession once a week. This is a grave disappointment to me.

Aside from this, the chapel is freezing. The uncomfortable wooden kneelers, not the prayers, leave a lasting impression.

After prayers we are herded along to the gym for the first assembly. Sister Minerva is on the stage introducing all the teachers with gusto.

Sister Minerva is the headmistress. Her face has a fierce, hawkish energy. Her smile has sharp corners, more like a grimace really. Although she's smiling, you get the feeling that if you did anything wrong you'd be on a sticky wicket.

Sister Minerva addresses the throng: 'What better way to start the new term than with a verse or two of the school song?'

A hunched and aged nun, the size of a small child, tinkles out an introduction on the piano. Automatically, everyone stands. (Is this the national anthem?) Tigs and I exchange glances. The school song is sung in earnest, each verse a bit louder and faster than the last. So by the middle there seems to be a race to finish the thing.

About twenty verses later, Tigs and I make our way to our classroom. As usual Tigs takes up a position towards the back and I, with my poor eyesight, sit at a desk near the front.

Next to me, a short blonde girl offers me some tuck. (For those who are unfamiliar with the term, 'tuck' means sweets, biscuits, cakes and the like.) She says her name is Lizzie Smith. She is as short and fair as I am tall and dark. Lizzie, it turns out, has the next cubicle to mine in the dormitory. Her parents live in Worthing, which is a nearby seaside town.

'Why aren't you a day girl, then?' I ask.

Lizzie shrugs. She is an only child. Why would anyone send their only child away? Lizzie gives me a whole Crunchie bar, so naturally I agree to be her best friend.

The first few lessons we spend meeting the school staff. Mrs Brown, for geography, is a soft glamorous American of about fifty, with dyed poodle-ish curls. Mrs Fitzpatrick, for history, is patrician, thin, not unkind. Miss Grafton, for science, is gruff, military-like, with possibly the worst basin-cut hairstyle in recorded history. Miss Best, for drama, is young, dark-haired and not wanting to be here teaching at all. Miss King, for maths, is white-haired and unintelligible. Plus, there is a bewildering smorgasbord of sisters, all with names beginning with 'Sister Mary ...'

We girls sort ourselves into 'chums'. Just how or why we are drawn to one person and not another is still a mystery to me. My core pals are Lizzie Smith and Sarah Corless.

Sarah Corless has curiously flat brown hair with flat eyelashes framing deep brown eyes. Sarah is smart.

Our team is sometimes boosted by the presence of Tigs and her new pal, Kate Lynn. Kate Lynn is by far the prettiest girl in the school. She has waist-length blonde hair and slanted, kittenish, sea-green eyes.

So there we are, sitting in the common room, huddled around a tepid radiator, swapping salient facts about each other: where we're from and what pop stars we like the best. David Cassidy, The Osmonds, Gary Glitter, The Sweet, The

Rubettes, Slade and Steve Harley and Cockney Rebel. You will be surprised to know that I am the only Steve Harley and Cockney Rebel fan. In order to educate my companions on the excellence of this music I sing them a few bars, '*Somebody called me Sebastian ...*'

To my surprise, they are not attracted by my singing, so we move on to the important topic of our favourite TV shows. *The Monkees, The Goodies, Top of the Pops* and *The Partridge Family*. We are pretty much unanimous in our tastes, which is a relief.

'*Jackanory?*' I offer. There is a brief embarrassed silence. *Jackanory* is a TV storytelling programme for young kids. Too late I realise no self-respecting teenager would mention it.

Television, it turns out, is not something we are actually allowed to watch at The Towers. Not even *Top of the Pops*, which is essential viewing for the teenager.

But, after insistent lobbying by all, Sister Minerva allows a bending of the rules. It is agreed that we can tune in to *Top of the Pops*.

'If there is any misbehaviour, girls, this privilege will be immediately withdrawn. There is also the proviso that if Pan's People appear, the screen doors will be closed. Such lewd dancing is inappropriate.' (The television is inside a lockable wooden cabinet, so we can hear but not see the action until the censored act is complete and the doors are reopened.)

This makes us all the keener to see *Top of the Pops*' resident dance troupe, Pan's People, in action. Fortunately, we nearly always cop a brief glimpse of them in the interval between a sister realising they're on and the time it takes to gallop down the steps to the screen to close its doors. This is except for the all-seeing, all-knowing Sister Minerva, who has reflexes faster than a cat's.

Saturday night is the highlight of the social calendar for the boarder. There is a screening of a film in the lecture theatre. This is a bit like going to the cinema, but in your dressing-gown and slippers. Unfortunately, the films are all selected by the nuns, so there's no chance of a roller-coaster ride of excitement.

To my horror, literature is also a strictly controlled and censored commodity at The Towers.

'All books must be stamped by the librarian and any books from home are to be checked with your dormitory mistress for approval.' Sister Minerva casts a look around the room like a minesweeper.

I keep my eyes down. Instinct and a certain amount of cautious inquiry have led me to suspect that Barbara Cartland novels would not be approved of. Hence the BCs are hidden in my locker. Barbara Cartland novels, especially the kiss-at-the-end bit, are high currency and can be traded at the back of the post office for 10p a copy.

My mother arrives for a visit. These have thinned out somewhat due to her having to visit Lu on separate days.

'How's Lu? How's Bud?'

'They send their love, dears. Lu's going to write.'

I nod. A picture of Lu all alone at St Joseph's flashes across my mind.

'Perhaps it's better that she's there than here,' I say to Mummy.

'Why? What's wrong with here?'

Tigs and I can't put it into words.

Mummy searches our faces, gives us a hug. 'It all takes adjusting to, give it a chance. Come on, let's explore.'

We go to visit the local attractions. Bramber Castle, as advertised, turns out to be not a castle at all as there is only one wall standing. But wait, there is more!

We wander down into the village to investigate the local museum. This marvel is called the House of Pipes, which is, surprisingly, just that. A front room full of pipes. Not musical pipes, mind, but tobacco pipes. Someone has spent their entire life collecting pipes. Personally, I do feel that if you have seen one pipe you have seen them all.

After the non-stop excitement of our sightseeing tour we adjourn to Ye Olde Bramber Tea-house. Tigs and I stuff ourselves. Mummy pushes a cake around her plate.

'So, have you made some new friends?'

I tell my mother about Lizzie and Sarah and Tigs tells her about Kate, but our conversation is awkward, almost as if between strangers. My mother fills the gaps with ordering more cups of tea.

She gets up and pays the bill and we walk back to school in strained silence. There's so much I want to say but I don't know how to start. At the school, our mother bends down to hug us and say goodbye.

'Mummy ...'

'Kathy ...'

It's too late, there's no time. Mummy's car arrives and the visit is over. All that's left is the fading day. Tigs and I trudge wordlessly up to our dormitory.

''Night, Tigs.' Tigs nods, I know she's feeling the same way I'm feeling, but she would never say it. Tigs never complains.

I linger at the window. There is a view over a thatched cottage. I look in through its lighted windows at its glowing fireplace and the family within. I wish with all my heart that I could be there, sitting around the hearth with a family. With my family.

I am invited by Lizzie to stay with her mum at their bungalow by the sea.

Because my mother is so pretty and glamorous, I am shocked to discover that Lizzie's mum is quite old and stout. More like a grandmother. Lizzie's mother has long grey hair like a witch. I don't feel comfortable with her at all.

She doesn't believe in turning the heating on, or giving you too much food, and seems to be living in a world of her own.

She startles me in the hall. 'Who are you?'

'I'm Kathy. You know, Lizzie's friend from school.'

'Ah yes ... Kathy.' She says it in a strange way, not warmly. I scurry into Lizzie's room.

'If you ask me, Lizzie,' I say tactlessly, pulling on an extra jumper, 'you're better off being at school.'

'Yeah,' Lizzie agrees, matter-of-factly.

'What about your dad?' I ask.

Lizzie shrugs. Lizzie's dad, like mine, has disappeared into the ether.

'He's dead, I think,' she says.

'So's mine, probably.'

Lizzie and I look at each other. Lizzie produces her compass and scratches the palm of her hand, making it bleed.

'What the …?'

'Now you do the same.' She offers me the compass.

'What for?' I ask, not really keen on the idea of pain.

'Because we will become blood sisters.'

'Okay,' I say. It seems like an important thing. I scratch my palm with the compass.

'Now we mingle blood,' says Lizzie solemnly. 'Now we are blood sisters for all time.'

Privately, I think that Lizzie's mother's ways have rubbed off on her daughter.

I catch the train home to spend the last week of the holidays with Mummy and my sisters. Tigs has already been home a week, and Lu is waiting for me too.

I'm surprised at how much Lu has changed in the months we've been apart. She looks so grown-up. How can I describe it? She's not the chirpy bundle she used to be; she's grown serious. More withdrawn. I feel somehow that I've let her down by leaving.

'Hullo Kathy.'

We hug each other, what else is there to say?

Bud stands and appraises me. She wears a remarkably groovy outfit: overknee socks, hotpants and a boob tube topped off by a smelly Afghan coat. She is the epitome of fashion. She punches me in the arm – some things never change.

'All right then?'

Mummy comes in bearing shopping bags. Goodies from Marks and Spencer's grocery section. She drops the bags in the kitchen and rushes in to hug me.

'Look at you! Aren't you growing up!'

My mother looks as beautiful as ever, her black hair tied in a glossy ponytail.

Over dinner, my mother looks at each of us. 'Isn't this nice? All together again.'

'Can't it be like this always,' I say.

'I wish it could be too, Kathy, but right now ...' Mummy tails off. 'Let's not talk about it and spoil our dinner.'

My mother has decided that Lu, Tigs and I need to make some local friends to play with in the holidays. She has been advised of a kid's disco party through the church. We are each to bring a Christmas present for the 'pool' – and we all get to take a different present home. Because I am easily as tall as my mother, she lends me one of her dresses. It has a shepherdess/gypsy look about it, with a twirly skirt, soft flared sleeves and a bodice. It is the prettiest thing I've ever worn. Tigs, of course, wears flared Oxford pants and a tank top. Lu wears a white maxi skirt. Even I have to admit, we look pretty ruddy groovy.

Mummy drops us off at four o'clock sharp. Our first 'disco'. We go into the church hall, a bit self-conscious. We are releived of our gifts and offered orangeade by an organiser in a safari suit. All seems to be going well. There are boys! Real boys! They stand in clumps, joking with each other and looking at us girls as we arrive. Furtively, I sneak glances at them, wondering what to do if I am actually asked to dance? I nudge Lu, who nudges me back.

The lights dim and the music starts. We start to dance. It's the one thing that I know I'm an absolute star at. I give it all my best moves; the boys are definitely looking our way. Suddenly, I feel a tap on my shoulder ... I spin around, twirling my skirt. I had imagined that it would be a boy about to ask me for my first-ever dance ... but no, it is a girl. A girl with an expression like she has been sucking lemons. This is a disappointment.

'You! Stop dancing!'

'Pardon?' I reply. 'Aren't we supposed to dance? It's a disco?'

'My friends and I don't like the way you're dancing.'

Sure enough, there's a bevy of local girls eyeing us uncharitably. We have stolen their limelight. Lu gives the girls a pitying glance; after all how could they possibly compete?

Another girl is unwise enough to tap Tigs very aggressively on the shoulder. Tigs without hestitating responds with a swift nutter. The girl goes down like a log. This is the signal, and twenty or so girls attack us. Tigs and I fight like billy-o. At one point, I am on all fours being bashed with several pairs of platform shoes (a seventies' hazard). By now,

I am getting quite angry, as the same girls are trying to rip off my clothes. I force myself through the crowd to the edge. All the boys are lined up against the wall watching. I appeal to them. 'Help us! Please help us!' The boy in front of me looks terrified. He says nothing. I realise that chivalry is dead or at least looking the other way. Tigs has managed to get to the edge of the scrum; we realise that Lu's not with us. We have to go back in to get her out. The thought that my sister is in the middle getting hurt makes me madder than hell. That's it, as far as I'm concerned. The gloves are off. Teeth, nails, fists, feet. I give anyone in my way sheer bloody hell. Somehow, we get Lu outside and the three of us leg it. After a while we stop to catch our breath. We are all of us battered and bruised, our clothes torn – but Lu, Lu is the worst. Both her eyes are beginning to close up and huge welts and bruises mark her little frame.

Back home, my mother is horrified. She takes one look at Lu's black eyes and calls the police. They arrive. The officer offers to drive us round looking for the culprits. We go back to the scene of the crime, but the place is deserted.

By ten o'clock, Lu, Tigs and I are all curled up in the one bedroom. Mummy comes to tuck us in. She is dressed up and her perfume wafts over us as she kisses us goodnight. 'Goodnight sweeties. Sweet dreams.'

She leaves. Bud stands in the doorway, her silhouette against the hall light. She is babysitting us. Bud doesn't say anything, just stands looking at us for a minute. I sit up in the bed.

'Where's Mummy going?'

'She's meeting Francis. She'll be home later.'

I nod.

'Go to sleep Kathy.'

From the lounge downstairs I hear Bud put on a David Bowie record. Though not an actual Bowie fan myself, I have become familiar with all the words to all the songs because we *have* to listen to it, over and over again ... 'Ground control to Major Tom ...'

The doorbell rings. I hear Bud go down the stairs to the front door. I hear her return to the first floor with someone. A male voice.

I creep down the stairs and peer into the lounge. Bud and a young man are cuddling on the sofa listening to records. So, Bud has a boyfriend. I crane my neck to try and see his face but the doorbell rings again. I scuttle back down the hall and listen as Bud goes to answer the door.

'Look, lady, someone called and ordered a taxi to this address ...'

'I'm sorry, but we didn't. We did not order a taxi.' Bud is firm, not intimidated.

'I've got it written down. To go to the cemetery ...'

'I'm sorry,' cuts in Bud, 'there's a mistake. No one from here ordered a taxi.' Bud closes the door on the taxidriver. I hear her lock the door carefully. She comes up the stairs and sees me.

'What are you doing up?'

'Is everything okay?'

Bud looks at me.

Is it just a fear left over from Daddy days? Something feels wrong to me.

'Is everything okay?' I repeat the question.

Bud nods. 'Don't be paranoid, it's just someone ordered a taxi and the address got mixed up. Go to sleep. Everything is okay.'

Round the Twist

Back from the holidays, Lizzie greets me as I come up the stairs. 'I've got something top secret to show you.'

I dump my suitcase and make a beeline for Lizzie's cubicle.

Sarah has already been bailed up; she rolls her eyes to tell me she already knows what it is about.

Lizzie draws the cubicle curtains and looks around secretively, then she rolls up her sleeve.

'What do you think?' she says.

At first I don't know what she's talking about, but then I notice she has printed some initials on her skin above her wrist like a tattoo.

'I presume LS is significant?'

Lizzie's face glows, like she's suddenly opened the door of the hot oven and got a face full.

'Leonard Smythe,' she beams.

I'm not with her, because I can't think who Leonard Smythe could possibly be. A member of a pop group? An American actor?

'No, dummy. He's my boyfriend and I love him.'

'What?' I say, floored. Boys are all very well in the mythological world of pop and movies, but in real life? A real boy?

'Surely he's not worth defacing your arm for?' Sarah says cynically, twisting a lock of her straight hair.

'Oh but he is!' gasps Lizzie.

I take a step back and look at my friend. Something has changed. Sure, she has grown a notable pair of bosoms but it's more than that. It's like a light has been switched on. She's all a-glistening and a-glowing.

'Leonard is wonderful. He's so good-looking. You should hear his voice. You know he goes to Rugby.'

On and on. My best friend's only topic of conversation is Leonard Smythe. We are stuck on the Leonard channel, until I find myself feeling jealous of this mysterious boy. I want my friend back.

That night I lie in my cubicle weighing things up. This Leonard business has unsettled me. Sex and the opposite sex are an unknown territory. On the one hand the nuns give you the impression that it would be better to die rather than have anything to do with a man, but on the other hand they make so much fuss about it there must be something to it.

There must be someone I can ask. What about my mother and father? They were in love once. Maybe I should ask my mother? Or Bud, Bud would know. But they are too far away.

I flick on my torch and look up the word 'love' in my dictionary.

1. Warm liking or affection for a person. 2. Sexual affection or passion — the relationship between sweethearts. 3. God's benevolence towards mankind.

Moving right along, I look up the word 'sex'.

1. (Some long-winded definition about being male or female.) *2. Sexual feelings or impulses, mutual attraction between members of the two sexes. 3. Sexual intercourse: to have sex with someone.*

There's also *sex act, sex appeal, sex life, sex-starved, sex symbol.* The dictionary contains quite a lot of words on it all, but not any really satisfactory explanations.

To distract Lizzie from her worship of LS, I put our names down for the annual Miss Towers Competition. This is modelled on the Miss World Competition, only without the swimsuits, evening dresses, high-heel shoes and all-round glamour. (The judges are nuns, need I say more?)

Sarah eschews such a mindless endeavour but generously offers to lend us her eyelash curlers. (Sarah has a fixation with curling things as her hair and eyelashes are iron straight.) I consult Bud's *David Cassidy Annual* that I inadvertently 'borrowed' during the holidays.

As Lizzie and I are quite different shapes I copy out the relevant style hints.

Tall and thin girls should wear blouses with puffy sleeves. Tank tops, maxiskirts, midis are flattering too. You're the sort of bird who should wear tent-shaped three-quarter-length jackets that break up your height and give an interesting effect.

Pleasantly plump? You'll look super in long tunic tops or outfits with long jackets to disguise heavy thighs. Never wear clothes that are too tight for you and only wear colours that blend naturally together: brown and tan, light blue and navy blue, orange and yellow.

Shortie? Garments with vertical seaming will make you seem taller. You look like a little China doll in floor-length dresses — why not buy more of them for the evening? You look best in tailored clothes; leave the fusses and frills to skyscraper girls.

Against this advice, I have decided to wear my new white ABBA jumpsuit, while Lizzie is going to wear her new glitter tank top with Oxford pants. Tigs generously lets me borrow her white plimsolls which, though smelly, match my jumpsuit perfectly.

The gym has been converted into a fashion showroom for the event. The rostrums have been pulled together to make a catwalk from the stage and a paper sign with the legend 'Miss Towers 1974' has been pinned to the curtains. Opposite the rostrum is the judges' table, overseen, of course, by Sister Minerva. The rest of the space is filled to the brim with giggling schoolgirls, with not a male in sight.

As the hour approaches it's a tight call to get access to any mirror in the building. We check and re-check our hair, our clothes and, most importantly, our knicker-lines.

Each contestant is to walk down the makeshift catwalk, turn, answer one or two probing questions from the judges and then walk back up to the stage.

'The eyes of the school will be upon you,' Sister Minerva says in a discouraging tone in her opening address. The old hunched nun at the piano tinkles out a hit song from the 1920s and the first girl launches herself down the catwalk.

My turn arrives. I step onto the rostrum and the lights from the photographers and spotlights are dazzling. (Actually, this is an exaggeration as there are, of course, no lights and no photographers.) I stop and pose to give everyone the benefit of my ABBA jumpsuit.

Then something takes hold of me and I start to twirl and strut and get quite carried away. The students start clapping, so I do a few more twirls and a bit of impromptu dancing. By the time I get to the judges' table I know I'm a star, better even than Twiggy.

Unfortunately, out of the corner of my eye I can see Sister Minerva frowning. This affects my confidence.

'Blessed are the meek, for the meek shall inherit the earth,' grimaces Sister Minerva. 'What on earth are you wearing?'

'It's a jumpsuit,' I say.

'Whatever it is, it is too small.' Sister Minerva waves me off disdainfully.

I turn and walk back up the stage with slightly less attitude. The crowd loves me, however, and I can't help but wiggle my way offstage, caught up in the moment.

I turn to Lizzie who is grinning at me, 'Am I all right?'

Lizzie gives me two thumbs up.

'Jumpsuits rule, okay.'

It's Lizzie's turn next. She sort of marches down the platform with her breasts leading and her short flared legs following. When she reaches the judges' table, she gives her blonde hair a defiant flick and flutters blue eyelids at Sister Minerva, who is as unmoved as granite.

'Is that make-up you are wearing?' Sister Minerva peers at Lizzie who assumes a wide-eyed and innocent look.

'No Sister, it's colouring pencil.'

'Well it looks ridiculous. Go on with you.' She waves Lizzie away dismissively.

Lizzie marches off, grinning at me all the way back.

The Miss Towers Competition continues.

'What do you think are the best qualities of a Towers' girl?'

'I think the best qualities are courtesy, respect and kindness.'

I look at Sister Minerva's face and see that she has swallowed this guff from one of the prefects who is wearing a neat tartan dress. Needless to say, neither Lizzie nor I win the Miss Towers title. We are far too 'in'.

The fine embarrassment of the traditional school play is alive and well in our corner of Sussex. After one or two bit parts in previous school productions, I decide to try for the big time.

Auditions for
OLIVER TWIST
2 pm today
Lecture Theatre

With the other hopefuls I sit down in the lecture theatre to await the arrival of our drama teacher, Miss Best.

Miss Best arrives theatrically late, waving copies of the play about. 'Here we are darlings … d'you mind sharing? Now let's get started.'

The audition drags on, several students vying for the parts of Nancy and Oliver.

'Now who wants to read for Fagin?'

There's a long silence and some shuffling of feet. No one but me, it seems, is interested in the part.

'Er, Miss Best? I would like to try for the part.'

Miss Best looks me up and down. 'I suppose you're tall, that's something.'

I present my singing interpretation from the film, 'You've got to pick a pocket or two', with appropriately miserly gestures.

When I have finished Miss Best sighs deeply and looks desperately around the room. There are no other takers. Reluctantly she gives me the part.

Our first rehearsal is dismal. Or rather I am dismal. Sister Minerva had popped in for a look and is now in earnest conversation with Miss Best. 'I don't think you can let her do the part. She's an embarrassment to the school.'

I sit there an abject failure, watching ancient Sister

Seraphim tread down the hall in her black cape and mittens. If only I had a black cape and mittens like that I could be Fagin.

Inspiration!

I gallop after Sister Seraphim who looks at me piercingly from under her snowy brow. She takes my hand in her mittened one and leads me to the top of the cellar steps where the nuns hang their spare capes and lets me pick out a long-ish one. Then she removes her mittens, delicately, one at a time, like a cat, and gives them to me with a theatrical raising of her eyebrow. 'Break a leg, young Kathy.'

Our opening night is a triumph. I am a sensation. No doubt about it. Helena Reeves says her father has taken my photograph and that I'm bound for fame and fortune.

After the show, I look in the mirror at my flushed, victorious reflection; orange make-up, talcum powder in my hair to effect greyness, waxy black eyebrows. I don't look so much like Fagin as a mouldy carrot. Still, it has been the night of my life. I have decided to devote my life to the stage. Up there, everyone loves you.

The next day, not to lose a moment, I begin writing off to drama schools to see if one will take me.

It is my week to triumph. Sister Minerva has noticed me! In English class the next day she says that later she will read out a poem I have written that should be eligible for the Platignum Pen Competition. I can feel the beams of jealousy radiate from every other student in the room.

I wait in semi-agony for her to recite my masterpiece. I wait and wait but, as the minutes tick by, I realise in horror that she has got caught up in actual teaching and that time is running out.

Sure enough, the bell rings! Oh, abject misery! My poem never sees the light of day. Until now, when I can redress this problem.

Painted Thoughts

With whispering silences I think
And within these thoughts are dreams
Dreams built of youth's bright faith and recklessness
They are rainbow-coloured wishes piercing the darkest
　　corners
With happy yellow sunbeams bursting forth into a fragrant
　　world
Filled with fountains of unknown joys.

Or my mind is peaceful in the lull
Of nature's breathtaking beauty
Here, my thoughts are painted with artistic care
In pastel shades sprinkled with a silvery mist.

But thoughts darken and down they must fly
To depths haunted by greens and melancholy blacks
Disturbing imaginings riding on crested waves of ruby-
　　blue
Flaming through crimson channels of blood and mystery
Down and down to a steely hell of despair.

But Faith, pure white Faith and hope
Gallant as a knight on the brightest steed
Drives back the darkest thoughts and hour
And with his brush, paints the light,
The pure white brilliant light.
All is well, the battle is won
... but the illusion lost.

While I am being indulgent, I should also like to mention this by Tigs. Possibly the only poem she is ever likely to write – she prefers to draw.

Lion

I am a Lion
With great big green eyes
Staring at the people with surprise
Eating meat with sharp shiny teeth
Walking along with plodding feet.

That night, as I snuggle down under my covers, I am thinking that perhaps The Towers isn't such a bad place now that I am used to it. Life is a different kettle of fish when you are in demand and popular.

Just as I am falling asleep, the shadow of Sister Minerva looms over my bed.

'Katherine, get up. Come quickly.'

This is most unusual.

I get up, put on my nightgown and follow Sister out into the hall. She puts her hand to her lips. We stand and listen.

Piano notes can be heard plainly, coming from downstairs. The notes are mournful and long. For some reason the hairs on the back of my neck stand up. I look at Sister Minerva; she looks disconcerted, not her usual confident self.

'Accompany me downstairs.'

I follow Sister Minerva downstairs to the piano rooms, which are situated on the first floor below the dormitories. Sister Minerva's bedroom is also on this floor, just by the staircase.

As we descend the stairs, the melancholy piano playing continues. We walk across to the piano cubicles. There are no lights on and it is pitch black. The notes stop.

Sister flicks on the lights and opens the doors. No one is there. In every cubicle we check the doors and windows. Nothing. By now I am completely spooked. What is it?

At the end of our ghostly tour, Sister leads me back to my dormitory. She doesn't offer any explanation. She crosses herself and I follow suit.

'Thank you, Katherine. Good night.'

I get back into my bed, my ears alert for the sound of a piano. There is nothing. I am vaguely aware of feeling honoured that out of all the girls, she chose me to come with her into the dark. Why me? Perhaps because I'm tall?

As I return to sleep, my subconscious is niggling me. It's not just the strange piano music. It's like a voice heard far off in a dream, something portentous. I know something is wrong, but I can't place it, can't put my finger on it.

The next day, Sister Minerva says nothing about our nocturnal inspection. And everything seems normal and bright in the morning light.

The Achilles Heel

'Kathy, is that you?'

'Mummy!'

'Yes darling, I've explained to the sisters that you're to come home and have your feet fixed. Francis and I have it all organised at the local hospital. Can you catch the London train up?'

I'm standing in the telephone booth where all the girls receive their calls from home. The subject of my substandard Achilles tendon is being discussed. This problem, it appears, is going to be fixed.

'Hooray! I can come home. Can Tigs come too?'

'No darling, I'm afraid not. There are important tests coming up, I'm told. So, just you for the week, okay?'

'Wooh-hoooooh!'

To my mind, and also because I have no idea what such an operation entails, it's a small price to pay to be going home. I am very cheerful. I run off to tell Tigs, who is playing tennis.

'Why can't I come?' Tigs sighs. 'It's not fair.'

155

'It's only for a week, Tigs – and anyway, you've got the tests. Don't worry, I'll be back in a week, unless I die on the operating table.'

Tigs stops bouncing her ball and looks at me.

'I suppose I should give you a hug then?'

Tigs hugs me in an awkward kind of way, and then thumps a ball into the net.

I run off to inform Lizzie, feeling a bit guilty about leaving.

Lizzie is deeply depressed. Her love for Leonard is unrequited. Several tear-stained letters have elicited no replies … or maybe he has moved?

'I hate to leave you like this,' I say. 'Will you be all right?'

Lizzie nods miserably.

'Cheer up,' I say. 'Tell you what, Valentine's Day is coming up and I'll send you a ton of cards from home, so you'll have more than anyone else in the whole school.'

Lizzie looks at me with her teary eyes and sniffs. 'Make sure you sign them with your left hand so no one recognises your writing.'

I agree.

At home, I am greeted by Francis. The sight of him shocks me to the core; he seems to have aged overnight. His black hair has turned grey and he moves slowly, like he's ill.

'What's wrong with Francis?' I accost Bud in her foul-smelling Afghan coat.

'Oh, he's had heart surgery,' answers Bud, tucking into a Cadbury chocolate. 'He can't eat anything fattening.'

'Why doesn't anyone tell me anything?'

That night, I plead with my mother for the details.

'I'm sorry Kathy, it hasn't been a good time and I didn't want to worry you. Francis has been sick but now he's on the mend. Go to sleep.'

She tucks me in and I fall into a deep dreamless sleep.

In the morning my mother takes me to the hospital. St Helier's is in Carshalton, a few suburbs from where we live.

'How old is she? Thirteen?' The nurse looks me over. 'She should be in the adults' ward.'

'Do you think that's wise?' asks my mother. 'She's not very … well you know … advanced.'

'Children's ward then. Come with me.'

We follow the nurse through the labyrinthine corridors of a public health hospital. Sights and sounds and smells accost me along the way: an old man coughing into a silver dish, a woman with bandages around her head, a baby with skin the colour of cheese, a man in a wheelchair staring out of a window.

'Take your clothes off and change into this gown. In a little while the Sister will come and prepare you for theatre.'

Mummy squeezes my hand. I'm not too concerned. What's a little operation between friends? My mother kisses me goodbye. 'See you later.'

I wake up from my operation to find the anaesthetist leaning over me, smiling. 'Hello,' he says, buoyantly. 'You've got a lovely pair of white boots.'

Still groggy, I wonder what he's talking about. He points to my feet. I look down the bed. Over my feet and calves are plaster casts. I do not recall it saying anywhere in the small print that I would have to have my feet in plaster.

'Does this mean I can't walk?'

'Not for a while.'

'Oh. What's a while?'

'A few months.'

There's always a catch isn't there?

Back on the ward, I fall into a post-operative doze. When I wake up, I think I am still dreaming as there are lots of little boys running around with no trousers on. There has been a job lot done in circumcision. The little boys' penises are untethered, with green blobs of antiseptic on, like mint ice cream. One of the boys, howling in agony, pees on my bed leg, leaving a puddle. The nurse comes and chases him away. She looks at me.

'You're awake then?'

The nurse lets me have a drink, but I vomit it straight back up, right down the front of her uniform. She is not thrilled. Caught between the boy's pee and my vomit: a great career, nursing.

My mother arrives with the most enormous box of chocolates to cheer me up.

As much as I would like to gobble the chocolates, I beg her to take them home, as otherwise I would have to share them with the nurses, ancillary staff and the circumcised boys.

I am in St Helier's for a week. I learn some important things from my stay in hospital. 1) There is life, there is sickness and there is death. 2) How to pee quietly in a bedpan.

Back at the flat above the beauty salon, my mother has made up my bed on the floor in the lounge. This gives me easy access to the guest toilet.

Francis hovers in the lounge room. We make slightly uneasy company, he recovering from his operation and I from mine.

My mother sits in awkward silence between us. There seems to be a coolness between them. It's obvious he is not comfortable with me being there, nor is she. After a while Francis turns his attention to his briefcase. He starts reading letters and signing documents.

'Francis.' It is the first time I've ever addressed him by name. He looks up slightly surprised.

'Yes?'

'Would you sign my plaster? You'll be the first one.'

For a minute, I think he'll turn me down, then his brown eyes look into mine and he smiles. He fishes for his fountain pen and signs his name with a flourish. I'm very pleased.

'Thank you.'

He has signed his name 'Franciscus'.

'Goodnight Mummy. Goodnight Francis.'

I'm tired, and as I drift off to sleep I see Francis and my mother sitting under the lampshade, almost like a normal mother and father. I hope that maybe one day that's what we'll be, a normal family.

The next day is St Valentine's Day. In the morning, half-awake, I hear the sounds of the house about me. The radio is on. My mother is making breakfast, bacon and eggs. Bud appears briefly in the doorway. Her skirt is way too short.

'Are you all right then?' She touches one of my legs in the plaster cast.

'Yes,' I say, still dozing in and out of wakefulness. Bud leaves for school.

A sound, like a car backfiring, wakes me up. I don't know why exactly, but I'm compelled by an overwhelming curiosity to look out of the window. I slide off my mattress and lever myself up to hang from the ledge.

The window is open and it is a sunny day. The tree opposite is in perfect blossom.

My eye is drawn down and I see a car pulled up in front of Francis's car. A man is in the street pointing a gun at Francis's head as he sits in his car. I'm astonished. I think that I must be hallucinating, but I am awake and this is real.

Perhaps I yell, I don't know. My mother runs into the lounge and sees me at the window. She runs over to prop me up and as she does so she looks out of the window too. She screams. Her scream startles me, frightening me more than the sight of the gun.

Hearing her screaming, the man with the gun looks up at us at the window. I don't recognise him, but my mother does. It's Daddy. My father gives a funny smile. The kind of smile you give before you throw up.

My father fires the gun again. I see Francis's hand moving inside the car. Does he lift his arm in defence? Blood splashes on the windscreen. My father fires again and Francis's arm drops. The windscreen shatters, and because of the shattered glass, I can't see Francis any more.

My mother and I fall to the floor like you see in the movies. She's hysterical, beyond reason. I crawl over to the phone and dial 999, giving our address, brief details. Then I drag myself back to the window to see what is happening. My father has disappeared.

On instinct, I haul myself along the hall to the top of the stairs to the front door. I see the flap of the letterbox lift. I know my father is standing on the other side of the door.

Everything is happening slowly and vividly. I anticipate, my body anticipates, bullets. Nothing happens. The seconds pass. I do not know why my father doesn't shoot. It seems an eternity before he walks away. I wait. Nothing.

I drag myself back up to the lounge. My mother is lying in a ball on the ground. At first I think she's been shot but she hasn't, she's insensible with shock.

I pull myself up to have another look out the window and I see my father standing by the car again. He reaches through the shattered window and fires the gun again. He stands so close to Francis that he must be almost touching him.

I scream from the window, to someone, anyone. 'Help! Help him!'

All of me wants to run, but I can't. I want to stop it. I want to go down and help Francis who must be bleeding to death.

As I watch, two men in overalls run up to my father.

'All right you – give us that gun.'

My father hands over the gun without a word, almost meekly.

The two men are mechanics from the garage down the road. Ernest and Richard Mower, ordinary men, but brave enough to face a stranger with a gun.

Bystanders start to gather, gawping at Francis in the car. I screech at them from the window.

'Help him! Help him!'

They just look up at me blankly, like idiots. I am filled with a furious rage and I drag myself back down the hall and down the stairs so that I can get out and help. I'm nearly at the door when the doorbell rings. It is the police.

I stand up and a nauseating pain shoots through my heels.

Letting the police in was a mistake. The minute they see me they refuse to let me outside to see Francis. My legs burn with the frustration of not being able to walk. I desperately want to go outside.

The local doctor arrives to treat us for shock. My mother is lying on the sofa in her burgundy satin dressing-gown. Her eyes are black. I tie my cross around her insensible fingers and say some Hail Marys.

From the window I see that the police have blocked off the whole area. The worst thing of all is that they leave Francis in his car out in the street all day, covered over with an old tarpaulin.

Finally, an unmarked van arrives; they pull Francis out of the car, his left hand holding his rosary. They untangle the rosary from his fingers and put Francis in a coffin and take him away.

A Curtain Comes Down

One by one relatives we haven't seen for years come out of the woodwork; the uncles, their wives, the cousins. They arrive in their Sunday best with their sympathy, and sit with their cups of tea and their opinions. The newspapermen gather on the pavement and the telephone rings off the hook.

All the time my mother lies like a dead person on the sofa.

At last Nanny comes, her white face lined with concern. I bury my head in her lap and she strokes my hair. 'Oh dear, Kathy. Oh dear.'

Bud arrives home from school, white-faced, her green eyes eerily bright. She sits between us, saying nothing. Lu, also, has been sent home from school. She holds my hand and puts a wet flannel on my forehead. We sit in the bedroom saying nothing.

Time drags on. The whole situation seems surreal. I look at the clock by the bedside table, the pile of clothes dumped on the end of the bed, the curtains, the mirror, my mother's hairbrush. All these mundane details.

Everything is the same – but it is not. This is death then.

'Things' go on but there has been a fundamental shift in our universe. A man is dead. Francis is dead.

The doctor comes and gives me a sedative, and I fall into a dark sleep. I think of nothing and I remember nothing. I wake in the darkness alone. I think for a moment that perhaps, after all, it's just a nightmare.

Early the next morning, although no one has consulted me, it is decided to send me straight back to The Towers.

Father Strahan of the Sacred Heart Church arrives to drive me back personally. He packs my wheelchair and a new set of crutches into the back of his car. Then he lifts me up and carries me down to the front seat. I don't see my mother, only Bud, who has tears in her eyes, and Nanny who is wringing her hands.

There are chalk marks on the pavement and that's how I know all over again that it is all too real.

When I arrive back at school there is a great fuss. The sisters come scuttling out of the front door in an unusual hurry. (Nuns seldom hurry, so you know something is up when you see them break into a run.) They bear me and my wheelchair up the front steps and leave me in the front parlour. I've never been in the front parlour before because, let's face it, you only go in there to be told a relative is dead. Just outside the door, I hear whispering. I think Father Strahan must be filling them in on the situation.

The door opens and Sister Mary Patrick comes in with a tray of jam tarts and a lemon drink. She gives me a sympathetic pat and goes out again.

Next Sister Minerva comes in. She regards me earnestly. 'I think it best, Kathy, if you don't breathe a word of what has happened to anyone. What's done is done and there is no point in distressing anyone unnecessarily.'

I nod my head. 'Yes, Sister.'

There is a problem getting me upstairs to bed, but it is solved by my sliding up the backstairs and along the floor on my bottom.

Lizzie and Tigs are waiting for me in my cubicle. They know nothing; as far as they are concerned I am just back from my operation.

'Did it hurt?' For a minute I don't know what they are talking about. I think of Francis dead in his car.

'Oh, my feet. My feet are okay.'

I tell them what happened. Tigs looks at me shocked.

'What's going to happen?'

'I don't know.' None of us know. We sit in the cubicle in silence.

That night I have the first in a series of nightmares. I wake up screaming.

Sister Maread leans over my bed.

'There, Kathy, there, there. "Suffer the little children to come unto me", why, Jesus would never let a hair on your bonny head come to harm.'

I look at Sister Maread and wish I could have my faith back. But I know, because I have seen it with my own eyes, that Jesus does not save you when someone comes to kill you.

Lizzie helps me as much as she can. She wheels me everywhere and waits for me when I have to go to the toilet. She is a true friend.

Unfortunately the shooting and associated details have been well reported in the press and Lizzie's mother decides that she doesn't want her daughter associating with me.

'I'm not allowed to be your friend any more.'

'But why?' I ask. 'What did I do?'

'My mother says you're a bad influence.' Lizzie won't meet my eyes.

'You don't think that, do you?' I implore my friend.

'No,' Lizzie looks at me. 'But I better go.' And she walks away down the corridor.

When I get back to the dormitory, her cubicle next to mine is empty.

On top of this, Sister Minerva has handed down her decision that I should take the mid-term tests after all. There was some suggestion that in view of my surgery and the trauma of what I had witnessed, I could be excused.

'Nonsense,' says Sister Minerva. 'It's far better that you have something to take your mind off things.'

I haven't heard from my mother, or Bud or Lu, and in the back of my mind I am constantly wondering what is happening. When I enquire, all the sisters will say is that it is better for me to 'leave well enough alone'.

On 8 March, three weeks after Francis is killed, it is Tigs' and my fourteenth birthday. In an effort to cheer myself up, I ask at the school office if I can order a birthday cake. The sister is about to place the order when she hesitates.

'Katherine … it might be appropriate for you to talk to Sister Minerva first.'

I accost Sister Minerva in the hall.

'Sister, can we order a birthday cake?'

Sister Minerva looks at me. 'Under the circumstances it is probably best if you don't order any extras until your school bill has been ... sorted out.'

I wander back down to the common room, disappointed and trying to work out exactly what Sister Minerva means. Slowly it dawns on me that now Francis is dead the money has stopped.

The implications are bigger than merely the lack of a birthday cake. Francis has paid for my school, my home, the clothes on my back ... I feel the chambers of my heart filling with a kind of choking despair. What is to become of me? Of us?

Francis's signature is on my plaster; how can it be that he is not here any more? How selfish I am. He has lost his life and I want him back so he can pay for my birthday cake. Tigs is silent on the matter. Even now, you won't hear her complain.

There is a poem by John Clare I learn by heart. It says what I feel better than I can myself.

I Am

I am! yet what I am none cares or knows,
My friends forsake me like a memory lost;
I am the self-consumer of my woes,
They rise and vanish in oblivious host,

Like shades in love and death's oblivion lost;
And yet I am! and live with shadows toss'd.

Into the nothingness of scorn and noise,
Into the living sea of waking dreams,
Where there is neither sense of life nor joys,
But the vast shipwreck of my life's esteems;
And e'en the dearest – that I loved the best —
Are strange – nay, rather stranger than the rest.

I long for scenes where man has never trod;
A place where woman never smil'd or wept;
There to abide with my creator, God,
And sleep as I in childhood sweetly slept:
Untroubling and untroubled where I lie;
The grass below – above the vaulted sky.

Tigs volunteers to come with me to the local hospital to
have my plasters removed. This is a brave move for Tigs as
she has an aversion to all things medical; dentists, doctors,
hospitals.

'It's the smell. The smell makes me sick.'

As for me, I actually like the smell of hospitals. I'm quite
looking forward to walking again.

The plaster-removing process hurts and I squeeze Tigs'
arm until she faints and hits her head on a radiator.

We are both wheeled out of the hospital a short time later
and collected by taxi. In my pocket is a chunk of plaster
with Francis's signature on it. In Tigs' pocket is a list of signs

to watch out for in case her concussion develops into a serious head injury.

At school I have to learn to walk again. The first time I stand up I can't believe how tall I am. I've grown used to a ground-level perspective. I wave around unsteadily like a giraffe on ice.

Unfortunately, due to the downturn in our fortunes, the physiotherapist has been scrapped. It hurts like hell to put my heels down, and I soon revert to wearing shoes with heels. Without physiotherapy, within a few weeks I am once more walking on my toes.

Tigs and I pack our bags. The school minibus waits in the drive to take us to the station for the train to London.

'Hurry up, or we'll miss the train. Put your cases in the back.' Sister Minerva is driving. She is as brusque as usual, and seems oblivious to the way in which our life at The Towers is ending.

Tigs and I get in, neither of us marking the event with words. The minibus gathers speed, but suddenly Sister Minerva swerves and brakes hard, barely missing Sister Maread who has dashed in front of the bus.

Sister Minerva barks out of the window, 'Sister Maread. What on earth do you think you are doing?'

Sister Maread, looking flushed and slightly embarrassed, opens the side door. 'Kathy ... er ... forgot something,' she says.

Sister Maread looks at me like she has something important to say. Only she doesn't say a word, but presses something into my hand. Then she turns away.

As the minibus drives away I look down. Sister Maread has given me a daffodil. It is yellow and bright and full of the promise of spring. A sign of hope?

So much for my optimism. When we get home, there is no home to speak of.

My mother has moved in with a young reporter from the local paper. His house is a two up, two down terrace in South London. The floorboards are ripped up and half the rooms appear to be in a perpetual state of renovation. My mum's new boyfriend is called Phillip. He is blond, boyish and likeable. His fair hair flops over one eye, he is very 'ex-public school'. His voice is a wonder to listen to, educated, light and so civilised. My mother is obviously smitten. Perhaps this love affair is her antidote to her recent miseries? As for myself, I feel as if I am hanging on to a capsized boat in a strange ocean. I don't recognise anything, even my own mother seems strange.

There is no space in the house, we girls feel awkward. Bud spends days at a time at her friends' houses. She seems to have handled the situation. She emerges now and then, wearing a boob tube or something equally ravishing. Bud has a job at a local jeans store. Now she's earning, she gives us money for sweets and ice cream.

Suburbia stretches out before us. The warm weather has arrived and the heat reflects up off the street The house is small and we don't have anywhere to go. Lu, Tigs and I hang around in the street. The kerb is lined with parked vehicles, hot metal glinting in the sun. Here and there are patches of vegetation, a few green-fingered souls conjuring a garden out of dust. Mostly, however, there are just fences and the 'I-spy' eyes of net-curtained windows. We play skipping in the street, but when we fall the concrete hurts our knees. There seems to be nothing. No comfort.

Tigs, Lu and I rescue an abandoned kitten from under a car; it is black with a white smudge of fur across its nose. As if to make up for our odd situation, my mother (and Phillip) let us keep the kitten.

We call him 'Sooty'. Lu, Tigs and I spend hours looking after Sooty, watching him tumble and play. It is a strange time. No one talks about what has happened, we just sit in the sun, playing with our kitten.

The situation can't continue, of course. Phillip is a gentlemanly sort but even we can see the welcome mat is wearing thin. My mother's passion is once more seriously compromised by the presence of her daughters.

'What do you think is going to happen to us?' Lu asks me. We look at each other. Tigs finds refuge in her silence. Her mouth forms a straight, grim, line.

'It's all a big mess!' I stab the ground with a stick.

'What are we doing here anyway?' Lu's voice is tinged with a kind of bitter despair. The life that we had, the security that Francis provided, has disappeared. Like the sinking of the *Titanic*, no trace has been left behind. Bud comes upon us, crouching, in Phillip's back garden, hacking pointlessly at the dirt. The debris of renovation is scattered on the ground, objects rusting and overgrown with weeds. Our kitten poos in the grass, the smell mingles with the heat and the dirt. I watch as the kitten, with his delicate paws, rakes the earth.

'What's wrong with you lot?' Bud frowns.

'We're fed up.' I say, half expecting, even now, a box around the ears.

Bud nods.

'It's all going to be back like before ... awful.'

'No!' says Bud, and she looks at us fiercely. We sit in a circle.

'Don't you see? We're safe, now. Mummy's safe now. Daddy is locked up.'

I look across at Lu, who is scowling.

'It's going to be all right.' Bud smiles 'You'll see ...'

I am not convinced.

'Yeah? How?'

'We're older now, we can get jobs, earn money ...' Bud is fervent.

Bud puts her arms around Tigs and Lu and me.

'We have each other, don't we? We'll help each other.'

Bud leans in, she leans in so close I can feel her breath on my cheek.

'... Besides you don't get it, do you?'

Tigs asks, 'Get what?'

'We're alive!'

Not Lemonade, You Fools,
Australia

The end of the story, inconveniently, does not come straightaway, it comes some twenty years later. Answers are sometimes a long time coming, if they come at all. This is real life after all, not fiction.

At eighteen I left England for Australia, hoping to start a new life in a land where there were no shadows. A land where you could see the sky and there was space enough to run. A land where you were not judged by your parents' deeds, only by your own. I worked: dish washer, waitress, sales assistant, photographic processor, receptionist, secretary – for a short joyous time I started a theatre company that went broke – then back again to a string of unsatisfactory jobs. Finally, I put myself through university, and began a career as a journalist.

At thirty-six years of age, I gave birth to Avalon. The excruciating, intimate pain of labour gave way to that perfect moment of birth. My daughter was and is a golden child.

As I gazed at her flawless, blissful face for the first time, a strange pain shot around my heart, like a band of iron. At first, I couldn't identify it. It was because I had become responsible for another life. In short, I had become a parent.

Like most new parents, I didn't sleep much. When I did sleep, my dreams were filled with ghosts.

In the small hours of the morning I would lie with my face close to my daughter's. I would feel her heart beat under my hand, her breath on my cheek.

To sleep as I in childhood sweetly slept, untroubling and untroubled where I lie.

A line of poetry appeared in my mind.

'Kathy!'

Was it my imagination or did someone call me? I sat up in bed and disentangled myself from the small child beside me. I told myself I must be hearing things. No one has called me Kathy in years.

I don't know why but I thought of my father. A father I had banished permanently from my thoughts. I tried to remember his face. I couldn't.

That morning, I watched my daughter playing with her father and I made a decision. The decision would upset my mother and sisters in England, but I was determined. I wrote a letter:

Dear Sir/Madam
    I am trying to locate, visit or find out any information

regarding my father ... He was incarcerated in prison for
a murder he committed on 14 February 1974. I have no
other knowledge of him, not even his birth date, and
wonder if you can help me?

When I wrote that letter, my father was already dead. He
had died alone in a hospital in London. He had called to his
nurses to take him to Australia. They thought that he was
delirious. They gave him lemonade.

Did my father call me in his last hours? I didn't know. I
didn't even know what I was looking for or why, I only
knew that I had to go back. I was a journalist after all. If I
could, I was going to get the questions answered.

The day before I was due to leave for England, I became ill.
Really sick. I was up all night throwing up. By four o'clock
in the morning I was positive that I would have to chicken
out and cancel the flight. But I didn't.

I got on the plane with my baby daughter. The flight was
intolerable. I slumped miserably in my seat, praying for
release. I have since formed the firm opinion that one of the
worst places to be ill is on an aircraft where you can't lie
down and you are surrounded by people.

It should be mandatory that all aircraft supply the
following: a) a children's creche, b) free aromatherapy
massages, c) a pool and barbecue area, and d) bigger packets of peanuts.

*

I also had another, more joyous reason for my trip. My mother was getting remarried once more at the tender age of sixty, and there was to be a family reunion.

You may be tempted to ask what had happened to my mother.

For the rest of her life my mother was never alone; she made a kind of career of men. She was always looking. Perhaps finally, happily, she had found a true love.

My sisters, like me, made their way through life as best they could. We worked at various jobs, good and bad. We always were each other's best friends, helping each other out along the way.

There the four of us stood, at my mother's wedding. On the surface you could say that time and distance had changed us; underneath we were just the same.

Lu wore exotic Indian pantaloons and golden bangles, looking like she'd stepped from the pages of *Vogue*. It sounds too simple, but she got a job in television and she did marry her rich man.

Bud used those keen green eyes as an artist. She was still in charge though, issuing orders to her husband – a sweetheart from our Raynes Park beauty salon days, and her partner in a sound marriage, too.

Tigs had also married and become a mother. She stood looking svelte and cool in a waistcoat and skirt. She'd spent the years giving her own children the chances she'd have liked to have had for herself.

As for, me, dressed in a red jacket and pinstripe leggings, I was the one still looking for something ...

My mother's wedding party was divided into two groups: the groom's side of the family and the bride's. Let us just say that the bride's side was less plain, including my mother herself, who looked positively girlish in a creamy lace creation. Her new husband appeared to be a gentle man, perhaps with a bit of spirit, as he wore spring colours against a sea of conservative grey.

Still not well, from my semi-delirium I watched as Bud organised the photographs, Tigs grinned and held her children's hands, Lu rearranged the floral display and my mother, shaking like a nervous child, said, 'I do.'

There we were, all grown-up, but underneath, still the same. The same kids who had laughed in dirt and held each other's hands. I glanced at the flowers. It was a beautiful day. The sun shone and clouds scudded across the sky of endless blue. Though not a sky as blue as Australia's.

After the wedding, the first stop on my fact-finding mission was to meet my father's last solicitor. Anita Bromley had kept my father's papers and she lived in Nottingham.

With my daughter on my back I caught the train north. At the station I was greeted by streams of football fans who flooded the train from end to end. It was impossible to find a seat. Seeking relief, I headed to the buffet for a drink. A mistake; the queue was a mile-long line of testosterone. I got heckled and fled, not up to my usual repartee. An observant steward took pity and got me a cool drink.

For the rest of the trip, I stayed in the corridor and on arrival ran off the train, utterly relieved. Behind me, the footie fans were in full voice '... you'll never walk alooone ...'

In Nottingham I scoured the shops for something to take to Anita. Desperately and pathetically – I was running late and feeling ill – I bought two bunches of flowers. It was an inadequate gift.

We took a taxi to Anita's address. The house was at the end of a long drive, lined with elm trees and separated from the street by wrought-iron gates. In its heyday it had been, perhaps, very genteel; now, it was a little neglected.

Anita looked younger than her fifty years. Her brown eyes gazed directly into mine. She had long, straight hair and a fringe, a child of the sixties.

She welcomed me to her rambling home and shared a generous lunch with me. We didn't talk until after the meal and her family had departed to the football game.

'I liked your father.' This was the first thing she said.

I was shocked. 'No one has ever said that to me about him,' I replied.

Anita laughed. She presented me with photographs. Photographs of me and my sisters as little girls. Photographs of my mother from years ago.

'These were on your father's cell walls. You know, I never heard him say a bad thing about any of you.'

I lifted my eyes from the photographs and looked at Anita. 'You're mistaken. I was told if I ever saw him again he would kill me, my mother and my sisters.'

Anita paused in thought for a moment, then said, 'I can only be honest with you, Katherine. I believe your father loved you all and that all he ever wanted was to see you all again.'

'Why did you keep all these things?' I asked Anita.

'I knew one day you would turn up and want to know, and I promised your father. We tried very hard to find you all, you know ... towards the end.'

Our eyes met.

'Thank you,' I said. It was inadequate.

Anita kept her promise to my father. She had boxes and boxes of his papers delivered to my sister, Bud. The boxes must have taken up serious space in my father's cell. Twenty-three years' worth. Yellowed letters, files, transcripts, newspaper clippings, photographs.

Bud handed it all over to me. She's not interested in digging up the past.

'It's not that I don't support you, Katherine. It's just that I support Mummy. Okay?'

Bud drove off, her knuckles gripping the steering wheel of her car.

That night I studied a photograph of my father as an old man. His face seemed at once strange and yet totally familiar, and the memories began to flood back.

'You're a good dancer, Kathy ... Dance for your daddy ...'

What was I looking for? I spent all night sorting through the papers and bringing back my lost memories.

In the morning, like the journalist I am, I had made a list of people to see and things to follow up. 1) Prison officials? Governor? 2) Kray Twins. 3) Friends (?) 4) My mother's relatives (brothers?) 5) Hospital. 6) Grave – where is it?

In London, Bud dropped me off at the Home Office. I had an appointment with a man called Malcolm Peacock, secretary of the Prison Officers' Association. I had brought him a bottle of Australian wine in thanks. He had managed to find and contact one of my father's prison governors, Muriel Allen.

Muriel Allen lived in Portsmouth, a nautical town. It's where the First Fleet set sail for Australia.

On the quay is a sculpture, three massive iron links, a chain that marks the suffering of those deported as convicts. I stood uneasily on the stone flags and gazed out over the grey horizon. My father spent many years incarcerated here, though he never got to see the sea.

Muriel Allen had retired and now tended to her elderly mother. Bravely, considering her past occupation and the people who might have held a grudge, she had agreed to meet me.

Her flat was in a tall building with a breathtaking view over Portsmouth harbour. Nervously, I waited outside her front door. I felt like I was about to attend an interview.

The door opened. Muriel was an impressive woman, a little intimidating. She reminded me of Margaret Thatcher.

'Katherine? Come in.' Muriel sized me up. 'First, let's have some tea.'

Muriel, kindly, had made up a pleasant afternoon tea. Salad. Sandwiches. Cake.

I admired her table, her view over the water.

'Let's have a look at you.' Muriel scrutinised my face in the light.

'First, you don't look anything like him ... except the eyes. You've got his eyes.'

This was a bit disconcerting for me.

'I'll tell you what I remember about your father. Remember, I was his governor, so I knew him in that capacity, that was our relationship.'

I nod.

'I was with him for over five years and I got to know him well ... as you do, day in and day out. Also he and I arrived at the prison at around the same time, that is why I remember him.'

I was riveted.

'He was about your height, slim and very clean. Always well turned out. He was always respectful. He never bucked the system or gave me any trouble. I feel very strongly that your father felt, "Okay, I did the crime and I am doing the time. Don't expect me to enjoy it but I will march through these days." Everyone in the prison community has a way of coping, of cracking it. Some turn to religion, some to education, others turn into health nuts – get big muscles. I feel strongly that your father felt he was in the right. That he found the situation with your mother intolerable, and did something about it. I feel that the key to the man is that he had his own view of the world and was single-minded. He was also a man who made you feel, "Don't mess with this man." Certainly he had a capacity for violence. But then, show me the human being who does not have the capacity for violence.'

Muriel passed me another sandwich.

'Then there was that whole libel case.'

'Libel case?'

'Your father sued *Penthouse* magazine for libel.'

'What?' I was all ears.

'An article appeared in the mid-seventies, an interview with your mother. Your father wanted to know what he could do about it. He was incensed about it. He said it was all a pack of lies. It was explained to him that the only thing he could do was to take a civil action against the magazine and that he would have to pay all costs, including the cost of getting to and from the prison under escort. Your father was not to be deterred. He said he would do it.'

'Where did he get the money from?' I asked.

'He had the money – the prison held prisoners' bank accounts and we had to ratify that your father could pay. People do have money in prison, even if they have committed murder. In my prison I had four millionaires.'

Muriel poured me a cup of tea.

'Do you know, I think that case kept him going. It gave him a purpose. The day came when he came back from the final court appearance. The whole prison was waiting for the news. Everyone was with him – the prisoners and the guards. "How did Ted do?" they all asked.'

'How *did* he do?'

'He won. He was quiet about it, not full of swagger, you know. The great shame was that he didn't specify an amount for damages, so they awarded him one hundred pounds, which didn't cover his costs.'

Muriel passed me a slice of cake.

'Your father had a great sense of humour. I remember recommending our education courses to your father. I said, "What about this? It's a great chance." He said, "No, thanks very much." I suggested art, and his response was, "That's for the poofters." But he must have gone away and thought about it, because he signed up for the art classes and to his surprise and pleasure discovered he was very good at it, so much so that at the end of the year he won a prize for it.

'He turned up one day with a package wrapped in grease-proof paper. He wanted to enter it into the following year's competition. The education officer opens the package and there is a painting of a lamb chop. See, it was one of the things your father missed from the outside. For every prisoner it's something different, for some people it might be pickled onions ...'

'Can't they have pickled onions?' I asked.

'Good heavens no! Vinegar is an acid, you might be able to erode a lock with it ...'

Muriel is passionate about her beliefs. 'That is why I was so keen on education. It's something positive in the prisoners' lives. Every year we would have graduation and we'd have the ceremony proper.'

'What, with gowns and hats?' I asked.

'Oh yes. With parents and friends, tea and biscuits which, alas, was all we could run to. Every year I'd make the same speech. We'd turn our backs symbolically on the prison, and I would say, "Today has everything to do with achievement, attainment and fulfilment and absolutely nothing to do with where it took place."

'That's one of the reasons why I can't agree with capital punishment. So much has to do with nature and nurturing. If capital punishment was a successful deterrent then crime would be no more. Judicial murder is murder just the same ...'

I looked at Muriel and in my mind's eye I could see the whole graduation ceremony, see my father getting up for his prize and the empty chairs where his daughters should have been, where I should have been.

'Did my father ever mention his daughters?'

Muriel watched me keenly.

'The only thing I can remember him saying is that he thought he would never see them again. Come on,' Muriel said, 'finish your tea, I've a surprise for you. I'm going to take you to the prison.'

It was a Victorian gaol, with old buildings around a courtyard. Kingston is a gaol for lifers; Muriel was the first female governor of such a prison.

We entered and guards escorted us though barred doors. Each door was unlocked and relocked as we passed through. I wondered what it must have felt like to be passing through those doors, knowing that you would never come out.

Muriel took me to meet the incumbent governor. We shook hands and they talked about the prison. My thoughts drifted away, my head still reeling from all the things I had learnt.

Afterwards we took a tour of the prisoners' courtyard. It was surprisingly pleasant. There were vegetable gardens, a green lawn, an aviary. Beyond, I could see the barbed wire on top of the walls and the narrow, barred windows. An old man was carefully tending a garden bed.

'Is he one of the prisoners?' I asked the guard. 'He seems like a sweet old man.'

'Oh he is, considering he hacked his wife to death.'

Murderers and Other Friends

I decided to track down the last surviving Kray brother. I wanted to leave no stone unturned in my investigation of my father. It took a few days to find out where the notorious Reggie Kray was incarcerated. I immediately wrote a letter to Wayland Prison. I understood that my father had spent the last years of his sentence at the same prison; what sort of coincidence was this?

Eventually I got a reply from Mr Kray himself. His handwriting resembled a series of slashes across the page and was difficult to decipher. Mr Kray said that he recognised my father from the photograph that I had sent, and that he was sorry to hear that he had passed away. He referred to the terrible 'family act' and wished me luck in my 'fight'. He also gave me a list of books he had written. As a PS he said, 'Be happy Katherine.'

Probably very good advice. I tried to arrange a visit, but the authorities refused me. They told me that Mr Kray was aged and ill and that even if I could get an interview, it would be a pointless exercise. 'Jesus himself cannot visit Reggie Kray at the moment.'

With this avenue firmly closed, I tracked down Mad Frankie Fraser, the Krays' right-hand man. He had spent forty years in prison, more than half his life.

I caught a taxi to Mr Fraser's abode, and as I stepped from the cab a head popped up from a basement, for all the world like the Artful Dodger on lookout.

'You Katherine?'

I nodded and offered up a few more bottles of Aussie wine.

We didn't go down the steps into the basement flat but up around another corner to a top-floor apartment.

His movements were furtive, and he kept looking up and down the road. Old habits must die hard and perhaps there were still good reasons for his caution.

When we got inside the flat Frankie relaxed. I took a good look at him. For a man of over seventy he easily looked decades younger. His hair was surprisingly dark and sleek. His tanned skin and his eyes inscrutable. Somehow he reminded me of a Native American. I was surprised to find I was taller than him and when I shook his hand, it was a surreal moment. Had he killed people with those hands?

Frankie had a wife, Marylyn, who was the daughter of one of the Great Train Robbers. Marylyn was blonde and sang in Frankie's stage show, 'An evening with Frankie Fraser'. You could tell that her life hadn't been easy, and I felt a rapport with her. Later, when we were alone, she asked me, 'How did you get out?'

Somehow I knew she was talking about the East End. About that whole criminal circle, and I knew without asking that she hadn't 'got out'.

I answered her truthfully. 'I ... I was kind of rescued,' I said, thinking of Francis. 'And then, you know, I saw what it did to my mother. I just decided to go the other way. I ran the other way.'

Marylyn nodded.

I gave Frankie a photograph of my father and he held it under the light. I scrutinised his face for signs of recognition.

'Abbott, you say?'

'Yes. He was in prison for murder, but before that he might have killed a policeman's son ... maybe in the fifties or early sixties. Would you have heard of it?' I think it was a newspaper article about Francis's murder which first suggested my father's involvement in the earlier killing.

Frankie shook his head. 'I'm sorry, love. I can't remember, he might have. A lot happened in those days.'

He looked at me with his dark eyes. Was my need so obvious? I could tell he was trying to be kind, and in a way I was relieved.

With no clear evidence that my father had been an associate of the Krays, I returned home. But that night I could not sleep, and I went back to the contents of my father's boxes. I sorted through papers. I was looking ... I didn't even know what I was looking for.

In my father's papers was a yellowed letter to a man called Thomas Barwick, at an address in St Paul's Cray. Something about the address was familiar.

In the morning I took a punt and wrote a letter, explaining my mission and that I was in England for a limited time. A few days later I was half-astonished to get a phone call in response. It was not from Mr Barwick but from his widow, Alice, none other than my parents' friend from my childhood. I arranged to go and see her that afternoon.

Black-haired Alice Barwick was now in her sixties, living in a tidy terraced house of the kind you find only in England. I brought flowers. She had one of her daughters with her. We sat in her front room with a cup of tea. Alice leant her head to one side and smiled at me.

'I can tell you that your dad and my husband were firm friends. They went way back together. They were of the same type, from the same place. You couldn't say they were soft men. They were hard.'

Alice gave the impression that her marriage had been just as hard.

'Did you know anything about … about their activities together?'

Alice shook her head. 'In those times wives were not told. You had your place in the home and that was it. It's not like now …' Alice nudged her daughter.

'I don't know how you stood it, Mum.'

We all laughed.

'Thank God times have changed,' Alice's daughter said.

Alice looked at me. 'I remember you girls. I was shocked when I heard you'd been put in a home. I couldn't believe your mother could do it. That's when all the trouble began. Ted began turning up here, night after night. It got so I was

sick of the sight of him. He kept going over and over everything, all the custody hearings ...'

'Custody hearings?'

'Oh yes. They went on for years. He'd turn up with the
papers asking what he should do. Then one day my
husband turned on the telly; the shooting was on the news.
He knew it was Ted. "He did it," he said.'

'Did he know my father was going to shoot Francis?'

Alice hesitated. 'I asked Tom straight, I asked him, "Did
you give Ted the gun?" and he denied it,' she said.

Ah, I thought. He did give my father the gun. I could see
in Alice's face that she thought so too.

Alice smiled. 'I'm glad you girls grew up all right.'

'Yes. Yes we did.' I answered.

'I've got something for you.'

Alice disappeared and came back carrying an old vinyl
record of *Jungle Book*. The very same record we had played
as children.

'I tried to throw it away, but my husband said, "No, that's
Ted's and his girls." He wasn't sentimental but he kept the
record in memory. It's yours, please take it.'

We hugged goodbye.

That night, I re-read the old documents, yellowing pages
that had spent two decades in my father's prison cell. The
papers smelt of 'institution'; they had that cold library smell.

It was ridiculous. I was supposed to be searching for
evidence, but here I was trying to conjure something out of
a sense of smell. Perhaps I was trying to sniff out my father.

I found a report written by Mrs Darling, the 'Avon lady' social worker from all those years ago:

... The family first became known to this Department in September following reports that the children were being left alone. Investigations showed that Miss Morris, then known as Mrs Abbott, had resumed work and was leaving the children during the day. Arrangements then were made to insure the care of the children whilst Miss Morris worked ...

Intermittent contact was maintained with the family and it was learned through the school that whilst Miss Morris worked Mr Abbott often stayed home and looked after the children. It seemed that he was fond of them and cared for them more than adequately.

In October, domestic quarrels resulted in violence and separation of the parties, and Mr Abbott's appearance in this court where he was given a six month suspended sentence. [For assault on the male neighbour.] At Miss Morris's request the children were received into care under section 1 of the Children's Act 1948. They were placed in a foster home and Mr Abbott was permitted to take them out. The children appeared very happy to see him and demonstrated a seemingly genuine affection for him. Mr Abbott responded warmly to the children and fully cooperated with this Department, returning the children punctually.

The following day Miss Morris forbade further contact between the children and their father, making allegations of a serious nature regarding Mr Abbott's moral character. In deference to her wishes the children were moved to a Children's Home and the address was not disclosed to Mr Abbott who has not seen them since that time.

Since the children have been in the Children's Home their mother has visited them regularly and also on Christmas Eve. Mr Abbott has written to the children on three occasions and the children have been encouraged to write to him. The Superintendent (of the home) reports that the children have settled without any signs of unhappiness.

The children have been visited by their child care officer on a regular fortnightly basis and are found to be forthcoming and talkative as individuals, each one readily able to make her presence and opinions known. They are affectionate, attractive and outgoing both as individuals and as a group. Bud the oldest appears to take the full load of anxiety and assured the child care officer that her mother had explained the reason for their placement and that she, Bud understood. Although the children have adapted well and may have taken to their stay at the home, a longer stay could well bring many problems to the surface. The children do not talk freely about their father and questioning brings evasion of the issue.

During the past nine weeks Mr Abbott has visited and telephoned the Department persistently requesting to see his children and asking for help in affecting a reconciliation with Miss Morris. He reveals himself to be a man who needs to surround himself with people who will reciprocate the attention he gives them. He states he has no friends outside his immediate family. Miss Morris would appear to be drawing away from the emotional situation in which she has been deeply involved.

Mr Abbott is a man who in his own way must have made a big contribution to the upbringing of the children. He repeatedly insists on his love for his wife and children and describes his parental contribution to the home as considerable.

The court will be aware that Mr Abbott has a predisposition towards violence in seeking his own ends and Miss Morris has constantly reiterated her fears of molestation by him. This makes a recommendation difficult. Nevertheless, it is felt that these children, with their unsettled background, and probable unsettled future, will need the support of both parents. Mr Abbott has in the past made a real contribution to the marital and emotional development of these children, and it is felt that access to them on a defined and limited basis would be in the children's interests, provided that no attempt is made by either parent to exploit the children and implicate them in the parental difficulties or that access is used by Mr Abbott to molest Miss Morris.

I also found pages of custody hearing transcripts, dated over several years. Perhaps the following excerpts are the most telling of all. The transcripts resonate with my father's voice:

In The High Court of Justice Family Division.
(In chambers)
Before Mr Justice Ormerod. Monday 24 July 1972

A: ... *while I was in custody she made arrangements and put them in care.*

Q: *Did you know what was going on?*

A: *No.*

Q: *Would you have consented if you had known?*

A: *Oh no, never.*

Q: *What did you try to do about it?*

A: *As soon as I found out, I went to the local welfare and they could see I was very unhappy and brought the children to see me immediately.*

Q: *And you saw the children then?*

A: *I saw the children straightaway and the two officers in charge were so amazed by the affection they showed that they immediately told me to take the children out for a few hours and provided I fetched them back at half past six of the night time that I could do so again the following day and every day until I had made my peace with what was going to happen between me and my wife.*

Q: *Were you in fact able to follow through with these arrangements?*

A: *No.*

Q: *Why?*

A: *I went there the next day and the welfare people said, we are very sorry Mr Abbott, you cannot see the children because they are not your children ...*

Q: ... and what do you do by way of a living?

A: ... I am not working My Lord, not because I am a lazy man but because this predicament has been over me for the last 2 and a half years.

Q: What has?

A: This thorn. This mental anguish.

Q: Yes I see.

Q: Have you received any treatment from your doctor?

A: Yes, I have been to the doctor and he has given me some pills. He said there is only one thing that will put you right and that is your children and he said, Of course, I cannot do that, but he said I can help you get a little sleep ...

Q: ... Mr Abbott you have been described as a man of violent temper, strong temper. Would you like to tell his Lordship how you feel about that characterisation of yourself.

A: My Lord, I am probably the same as any normal man is, put to the trial and tribulation that I have been put to. For the past two years all sorts of lies and deceit had been going on behind my back. It becomes at times intolerable and I do not think that I am any more violent than any normal man placed in the same circumstances.

Q: ... what about this prostitution. This (Escort) call girl business?

A: It was a complete surprise.

Q: The situation is not that you forced her to go out?

A: No such thing.

Q: And that you beat her if she did not?

A: That is a blatant lie. I never touched her.

Q: And that you brought her to the West End in your car?

A: That is a blatant lie.

Q: And collected her in the early morning?

A: They are blatant lies.

Q: Is it not correct that in the last two years you were living with Miss Morris you did no work at all?

A: That is incorrect.

Q: So the witnesses are lying about that too?

A: Yes.

Q: In the last two years that you were living together with Miss Morris, (the witnesses) say you were having a period of prosperity ... You had plenty of money to spend.

A: Well I would not say that we were prosperous. I would say we were getting a living. I would say that probably Miss Morris, as she now is, was prosperous on her own behalf because she knew the money that she was putting in the bank on her own behalf.

Q: The family had a holiday in Bournemouth for instance did it not?

A: Well that's not exorbitant is it?

Q: Do you complain that the arrangement for the children is unsatisfactory?

A: What I complain about is my separation from them.

Q: You want to see them, that is the only thing? If you

heard that the children would be upset by seeing you would you still wish to see them?

A: *If I heard that the children would be upset by seeing me, it would amaze me to see my children upset if they see me, it would amaze me.*

Q: *They have struck me as being distinctly upset at the thought of seeing you ...*

A: *My Lord you are basically a just man ... You must know basically I am an honest man. My children are my life ...*

Q: *I know, but at this point we cannot go backwards.*

A: *No, but I feel this Francis who she is co-habitating with now, he is a married man with nine kids. I cannot tolerate this My Lord.*

Q: *What cannot you tolerate?*

A: *I cannot tolerate the children's mother acting like she is acting.*

Q: *None of us can help you about that.*

A: *No but surely everything has been done in her favour. The children have been made wards of court. I mean she still sees them. If she loved my children she would want to be with them all the time. As it is she only sees them some of the time.*

Q: *She has got one of them with her now hasn't she?*

A: *Only the oldest one, because the oldest one, you know, probably wants to be with her mummy. They all want to be with their mummy. I have never turned my children against her.*

Q: Surely the children themselves are perfectly happy.

A: They are happy children because I brought them up happy.

Q: All the more credit to you that they are happy children.

A: They are my own children, my own flesh and blood. I haven't left her, she has left me.

Q: No. No. I am just telling you that the children are happy.

A: Yes but I am unhappy.

Q: You are unhappy?

A: I am the unhappiest man in the whole wide world.

Q: I'm sure you are. I understand.

A: I would hang for that woman and she knows it.

Q: Well I would not say that. I would not say that if I were you.

A: This is my loyalty to her. This man, paramour, put the pressure of money on her. I blame him more than her because of this weight of money …

Do you think I should be deprived of my children because of her whims and because of a rich man's whims. He wants a bed mate.

Q: If you approach it like that Mr Abbott I will go the same way with you. I will not have it.

A: I am not going to row with you. Look what I am saying is these children, I love them. Look why cannot I see the children with you in your chambers?

Q: Because it will upset them too much. I am asking you to help me let them get settled for a year.

A: They will never know me in a year.

My father wrote endless letters:

I am the father of the four girls that attended your school from the 70s onwards … I have made protests to the courts about this unfair and diabolical set up, my separation and of being denied access to my own children — their kidnapping and the alienation of them against me by various court actions through disreputable solicitors and other legal persons … and I am still right up to this present day trying desperately to see my children. To see my daughters who are growing up …

I do believe that my father, in his own unyielding way, did love my mother and that, paradoxically, though my father was living off my mother's earnings, prostitution destroyed their relationship. He was jealous. My father ended up with little self-respect.

Although he had only himself to blame for the situation, he decided that he would blame someone else and that person was Francis Van Seumeran.

From an original statement to the police in 1974:

I went to Raynes Park as I had found out where Marie was staying. In a flat over a beauty salon. Her own salon. He must have a lot of money to spare to buy her a whole business and a flat mustn't he? I took to watching the place, to driving past at all times. I never saw the children, only a glimpse of Bud once, when she went to school. I don't know where the others were. I'd see Marie coming and going. It was all I could do not to get out and talk to her. But I knew she'd call the police. Then one day I was passing there and I saw the 'For Sale' notice outside. I was scared because I thought they were going to clear off with my children. I was in a state of panic. I had taken to waiting at Gatwick and Heathrow airports on the off chance I would see her paramour, Van Seumeran, passing through. On the 13th of February I checked all the flights from Amsterdam and Rotterdam but I did not see Van Seumeran. Mind you, I didn't know what he looked like so I was up against it. I only knew what his car looked like. I hoped something inside me would tell me that was him. I wanted to know why he would never speak to me. Why he ignored my appeals. I went back to Marie's. All the lights were on, so I waited around for a bit in the hope of seeing this Van Seumeran, but it was late and I was tired so I thought I would go home and wait and see him the next day. On the way home I called at a friend's and after a lot of persuasion he lent me a gun. I wanted to impress my torturer, Van Seumeran, with it. So he would listen to me.

I didn't sleep much that night. I got on the road early to make sure Van Seumeran's car was there. At this stage I still had not seen his face. I did not know what he looked like. A man in a good suit walked to Van Seumeran's car and got in, I knew it was him. I drove my car up to the side of his car, and got out. He looked at me.

*At first, I could see he wasn't certain who I was. So I told
him. Then an expression crossed his face like, 'Ah, so this
is the piece of dirt, is it?' I asked him why he was stopping
me seeing my children and then he told me to 'Get out of
the way' and drove his car at me. I jumped on the bonnet
and I was shouting at him to stop, to look at what I had
in my hand. I was sure he would listen. He must have
thought it was a toy. I thought once he had seen the gun
he would stop and talk but the man was a fiend. It was
unbelievable. I had not bargained on him acting like
that. He was in a superior position. He worked me up to
a pitch and I lost control.*

*The car window was shattered, I could practically
touch him. I could see him looking at me. I pointed the
gun at his forehead, I was looking into his eyes and he
mine. He looked like he was praying, like he knew this
was his last moment. He didn't plead or cry or anything
like I expected.*

*I saw Marie and a girl, later they said it was my
daughter Kathy, at the window. She was screaming, 'He's
dead.' After that the police arrived and took me off.*

My father shot Francis six times. Once through the arm,
twice to the shoulder, and three times in the head. The
whole thing took about ten long minutes. As Francis lay
dying, he managed to take the rosary he always carried from
his pocket. The police removed it from his fingers. I hoped
his family got that rosary.

*

My father's trial was a one-sided affair, with evidence only from the prosecution. There were no defence submissions. The records show that my father received the following sentence:

> *Unlawful wounding – 5 years' imprisonment*
> *Unlawful wounding – 5 years' imprisonment*
> *Carrying a weapon with intent to endanger life – 15*
> *years*
> *Murder – Life imprisonment on conviction for*
> *manslaughter on grounds of diminished responsibility.*

There was no explanation of the finding of 'diminished responsibility' within the papers and I have not been able to obtain a satisfactory explanation from any other source.

The 'unlawful' woundings refer to stray bullets that inadvertently hit two passersby. I have not been able to trace these men, but newspaper reports of the time indicate one was a young lorry driver who required a short period in hospital to recover from leg wounds, and the other was an elderly gentleman who received a superficial chest wound.

My father's ultimate punishment was not his prison sentence; after all, he had killed a man in cold blood. It was the final and irrevocable loss of his children.

Like many children confronted with murder, my sisters and I turned our backs on the murderer. We were told by my mother that he would do us harm, that we were in danger. I don't believe now that this was true. My father never had any intention of killing his children. But this belief kept us away, kept me away. I was afraid.

My mother set up a meeting with a lawyer and we children wrote the following statements:

8 September 1977
I myself, Miss Tigs Abbott will not and shall not ever consent to see my so called father Mr Edward Abbott ever again in my life, this is my entire and solemn wish, I shall have no change of mind.
Written by
Tigs Abbott

I do not wish to see, speak or make any further contact with Mr E Abbott now or in the future.
Lu Abbott (Miss)

I do not wish to see, speak to or correspond or to have any contact at all with my father.
Bud Abbott

I have no wish or desire to contact or see again, my father Edward Abbott. Furthermore never to be troubled by him in any way whatsoever by any means available to him.
Katherine Anne Abbott

A Three-legged Table
Finds Its Own Balance

In this age, when killing has become an entertainment, murder is a contaminating disease that affects our whole society, like ripples in a pond. If I could go back and sit my father down, I would tell him: 'Don't do it.' I would give him this list; maybe I would give any desperate person considering killing someone this list:

1) If you seek revenge, dig two graves. One for yourself.

2) Forget how the news media represents prison. Prisons are sad, soul-destroying, torturous, barren places. The worst places on earth that anybody would want to be.

3) You will destroy and/or lose *any* relationships you have now; with your partner, your children, your friends, your family. You will also destroy not only your victim's life but the (innocent) lives of your victim's family.

4) After this, you will never be happy again.

5) Outside in society you will cease to exist or even be remembered.

*

Perhaps by guilt, I am drawn again to my father's documents. What am I looking for? Some sign of redemption? I don't know, and I am running out of time.

I seek out a prison volunteer, one of many kind people who visit the unvisited.

On the Underground, I recognise the names of places from long ago: Piccadilly Circus, Leicester Square, Covent Garden. It all seems surreal.

As a reality check, I look round at my daughter; she's in my backpack clutching the handrail as if she's been 'tubing' it all her life. She blows bubbles at the hardened commuters, and even they are forced to smile.

Mr Francesco Lurati meets us outside the tube station and drives us to his home. My first impressions are of a quiet and elegant man. He is in great shape for a man in his seventies.

He lives on a hill overlooking the north of London. His rambling house is filled with wonderful paintings. He points one out to me above the fireplace.

'That is my father's. He painted it to commemorate one of his sons who died as a baby.'

The painting is, to my eye, a masterpiece. A toddler, asleep, is tinged with blue and draped with a single chain of flowers as he ascends heavenwards. The emotion, the pain, the silence, are clearly evident in the painting.

'It's beautiful,' I say.

'We come from a long line of artists. Myself, I restore stained glass, mostly in churches, though I am retired now.'

Francesco's diminutive wife, Delfina, invites us to lunch.

'How did you know my father?' I ask.

Francesco smiles, 'I was what you call "a compassionate volunteer" – I was interned in the war and I remember what it was like. That's why I visit and that is how I met your father.'

This statement makes me feel enormously guilty. I, the daughter, should have been the visitor.

'I knew your father for the last ten years of his life … I keep a diary and I've transcribed my entries from the days I visited your father. Maybe it will be of some help …'

Francesco passes me a notebook.

I scan the first entry quickly:

Saturday 14 October 1987.
Prison very grim. Great thick walls. Perhaps 20ft high with a rounded metal top so that one could not get a grip or use a grappling iron … The prisoners were brought in: blue striped shirts, dungarees, blue jackets …

… Ted Abbott, a slim upright man aged 67, looked quite fit … A cockney from the East End but very articulate with a sense of humour. A pleasant fellow. Has been 'inside' for 14 years even though he was found guilty of only manslaughter, seems to have little chance of parole. Perhaps this is not helped by his not kowtowing or crawling to anyone. He even insists on the woman governor calling him 'Mr Abbott' and not 'Ted'.

And another page:

9.15. Left for Wayland Prison ... Usual procedure. Ted's 68th Birthday. Pleased to see me. I often wonder why I go, but once there, it seems worthwhile. He gave me some of his watercolours, mostly of flowers, very good. Home 18.45 ...

Francesco talks about my father and his relationship with him. How he continued to visit and assist my father through his final years.

Later that night I reflect on what he has said. I spread the papers of my father's life about me: his drawings, snippets from prison life.

To His Right Honourable Her Majesty's Principal Secretary of State for the Home Department ...
My petition concerns the change of practise as it applies to me with regard to the town purchase facility as operated through the prison canteen. I do not smoke, I am unable to take part in sporting activities and I have no means of listening to records or cassettes. Consequently it has always been my pleasure to spend my earnings on food. For this reason I like to choose particular commodities I prefer. Such as Brooke Bond PG Tips tea bags, Anchor Butter, McDougals Self-Raising Flour, Walls pork sausages ...

And the boxes and boxes of letters reveal his years of effort in trying to obtain some contact with his children. He never gave up, and as illness took hold in his final years he became desperate. Advertisements appeared in the local paper:

ABBOTT FAMILY
Would anyone knowing the whereabouts
of Bud, Tigs, Lu or Kathy Abbott
last known of Durham Rd, Raynes Park
and Wimbledon please request them to
contact: 01 858 3534
On a matter of the greatest urgency
in the strictest confidence

After a telephone call to a Mr Richard Warren, a kindly bereavement officer, I am furnished with the date of my father's death and also his birth date, which I had never known.

Francesco takes me to see the hospital where my father died.

'Go inside. See what you need to. I will wait here.'

Dr Ali, of Greenwich Hospital, a Pakistani gentleman in the truest sense, retrieves his medical notes and spends some time with me going over the drawn-out death of my father. A deteriorating struggle for breath, a chronic disease of the airways.

I am also able to meet the nurse who was on duty the night he died. A part of me is hoping that my father had some last words, something meant for me. The nursing sister is chubby and African, with one of the kindest, most compassionate faces I have ever seen. I immediately think: 'If I were dying, this is a face I should like to see.'

She goes over my father's last moments with me. He died overnight, with no last words. 'He just went ...'

She wraps me in her big arms as I begin to cry.

'I lost my own father, I know what it's like,' she says.

My emotions are all confused. Am I crying because there were no last words for me, Katherine? Or is it because I am finally stricken with the natural grief of losing my father?

Outside, Francesco has waited patiently for hours.

'Thank you,' I say, through my tears.

The next day, I turn my attention to the family of Francis Van Seumeran. I find out from police records that one of his sons identified his body. I think of what it must have been like to find out not only that your father had been murdered, but that he had lived a double life with another woman.

I make calls to Holland trying to locate the family, but in the end I am unable to find a Van Seumeran.

It was perhaps Francis Van Seumeran who saved me, who lifted me into a lifeboat for those few crucial years. If there are any heroes in my story, then perhaps he is the one?

I have one last stop. My father's grave. He is buried in the cemetery in the shade of Shooters Hill.

The cemetery is pretty, shadowed by a small church. It is a sunny day, insects buzz over the tombstones, the sky is blue. Francesco shows me the place where my father is buried. I ask to be alone.

I am alone at last with my father. After all these years it is too much. I fall to my knees and I want to touch him, to reach through the ground and pick him up in my arms. I am crying. I am crying for myself, for my mother, for my sisters, for all the terrible things that happened. I am crying for the suffering, for the lost years and the mistakes we all have made. I realise that my adult heart contains the child-heart that loves who it always loved, right from the begin-ning and right to the end. And that child heart is accepting and understanding and forgiving.

That night, I sit with my father's life around me. I begin to pack the papers away when my eye falls on a faded report.

> *She (Bud) has good recollection of her earlier years but agrees that Lu would not as she was too young. Her impression is that her father (the plaintiff) made much of Lu and to some extent herself but did not appear to like Katherine and showed it.*

Ah! This is it. After all I've been through, this little scrap of paper is what I have been looking for. It's clear to me now that I have been searching for proof that my father loved me. I shake my head. I can even laugh. At last it is all over.

Picture, then, if you will, that small child with greasy brown hair and an eye-patch. The child is concentrating hard, the tip of her pink tongue compressed between her lips for added concentration. She is working out how old she will be at the start of the new century. She figures the numbers laboriously, rubbing out calculations with her eraser and starting over again until she gets it right. To the child, it seems impossible that she could ever be so old.

Picture, then, the woman the child has become. The same brown hair. A tall woman, who walks along a sunlit beach in a sunlit land. Her children skip beside her. You can see their footprints in the wet sand. Where they have come from, where they are going. The journey they have made.

Acknowledgements

My love and gratitude to my dearest sisters, my life-long companions who have enriched my life beyond all measure.

To my friends: Irma Havlicek, Adrian Bortfield, Richard Browne, Yvonne Celia, Susan Collie-Lyall, Sarah Corless, Kate Lynn, Rita Clarke, Peter Pakula, Jan Petite-Lawson and Geraldine Mellet.

Alex Morcos, the Haran family, the Sisters of St Joseph's Dominican Convent, the Convent of the Blessed Sacrament (The Towers), Franciscus Van Seumeran, Anita Bromley, Francesco and Delfina Lurati, Muriel Allen, Malcolm Peacock, Richard Warren, Dr Ali, Bill and Ray Morris, the John Clare Society, Greg Smith, Jenni Garrigan, Candy Baker, Janette Young, Alan Payne, John Beaton, Claire Dobbin, Barbara Mariotti, Sylvia Wilczynski, Amon Rynne, Warren R. Burns, Mark Firth, Dianne Smith, Jenny Williams, Glynis Hickford, the students and staff at Rossmoyne SHS and North Lake Senior Campus, Dr Sandra Parsons. Sir Clive Newman, Sir Ray Coffey, Susan Murray, Wendy Jenins, Leone Dyer, Nyanda Smith, Helen Kirkbride and all at Fremantle Arts Centre Press; Charlotte Cole of Ebury Press.

– For their support and encouragement.